GROWING PROFITS

HOW TO START AND OPERATE A BACKYARD NURSERY

MICHAEL AND LINDA HARLAN

Moneta Publications, Citrus Heights, California

Growing Profits
How to Start and Operate
A Backyard Nursery

Michael and Linda Harlan

Published by Moneta Publications, Citrus Heights, CA 95610
Printed by Griffin Printing, Sacramento, CA
Cover by Creative Factory, Sacramento, CA

Library of Congress Catalog Card Number   96-94865

ISBN 0-9654567-4-9

Acknowledgments

We wish to thank TLC Polyform, Inc. for permission to reprint illustrations of their containers; the McConkey Company for the drawing of shade cloth on pole and cable frame; Western Pulp Products Company for permission to reprint their clip art showing plants in biodegradable pulp pots and Nursery Supplies West, Inc. for their permission to reprint illustrations of their containers. The Scotts Company and TLC Polyform, Inc. provided distributor lists which were used in Appendix Two.

DISCLAIMER

This book is designed to provide information in regard to the subject matter covered. It is sold with the understanding that the publisher and authors are not engaged in rendering legal, accounting or other professional advice. If legal or other expert assistance is required, consult the services of a competent professional. Nor are the authors endorsing the use of any particular product or brand or suppliers.

It is not the purpose of this book to reprint all the information that is otherwise available elsewhere. Consult other works for more specific information on the particular types of plants you intend to grow.

The text is to be used as a general guide not as the ultimate authority. Rules and regulations on growing plants not only vary widely throughout the country but also change and it is the reader's responsibility to confirm with local authorities the legal requirements for going into business and operating their nursery.

TABLE OF CONTENTS

INTRODUCTION

Following a Take Your Daughter to Work Day intended to promote greater awareness of the workplace among young girls, a cartoon appeared showing a girl riding home in the car with her mother who was asking her what she had learned. "I want to be self-employed," was the response.

Whether we need to earn a living or just want some extra spending money, what we all want most is employment we can enjoy under our own terms. Work done on our terms hardly seems like work at all. Gardening is one form of labor which has become a pleasurable pastime. Many who pay professional gardeners to mow their lawns and trim their shrubs, reserve for themselves areas where they turn their own soil, plant their own flowers and tend their own trees. This is no longer work, but fun and relaxation. Any marriage between a fun, relaxing pastime and a business operated on one's own terms may seem an elusive dream, but it is waiting for you in your own backyard.

The authors have made their living for over a decade growing plants on a one-half acre parcel of land.

CHAPTER 1

MAKING THE TRANSITION FROM GARDENER TO NURSERYMAN

Gardening has become America's favorite pastime and meeting gardeners' needs for plants and supplies has turned the nursery business into the second-most important sector in the U.S. agricultural industry. All the basic pleasures of gardening are to be found in the business of growing plants. Indeed, the production of much plant material for sale is really only container gardening for profit. This book is written for the person who wants to take the love of gardening that extra step to gardening for profit.

Most gardeners are familiar with the retail end of the nursery business. However, in many cases, the retail nursery produces few or none of the plants that it sells. Wholesale nurseries are the major growers and suppliers of plant material to the industry, and these operations are very different from what the gardener is familiar with on the retail level. Whether gardeners are buying seeds, or starter plants, or mature specimens, they have little or no contact with the production end of the industry; yet it is this aspect of the industry that is closest to the very nature of gardening.

The object of retailing is to buy a product and resell it at a higher price. The goal is to turn the product quickly. The quicker the money turns, the greater the profit potential. Retailers are not anxious to watch a plant grow, they just want to see it go. The longer it sits in their nursery growing, the longer their money is tied up.

Wholesale growers are business people who are just as anxious to realize a profit. But they are the ones who are truly interested in seeing the plant grow, for the faster the plant grows, the faster they see their profit. The gardener, then, has the greatest affinity with the wholesale grower. Both share the same pleasures: to watch a plant start from a seed and push its first leaves up through the soft dirt, to see the thin stems grow strong and leafy, to see the plant bud and burst into color, to experience the cycles of nature and to feel that primeval instinct to work the earth and to enjoy its harvest.

Considering the capital investment you see in the commercial nursery, the land, the equipment, the inventory, you may wonder how you can afford to get into the nursery business. None of these things are obstacles to starting your own nursery. If you have room for a garden, you already have the land. If you have a shovel and a hose, you have the basic equipment, and after buying a few supplies such as nursery containers, fertilizer and soil, you can produce the inventory. Until the moment that you actually sell the plant, you are only gardening; it is the selling that puts you into business.

The advantage of this particular type of business is that by doing something you already enjoy, you can generate extra spending cash working only the hours you want, or you can put in more time and provide your whole living with a pleasant job you can do at home.

Developing a business from your hobby is frequently just a natural progression. Growing up on a farm on which his parents raised fruits and vegetables, Dick Wood of Newcastle, California started gardening when he was two years old. But he never saw it as a way of making a living. Although Dick preferred a career as a junior high school science teacher, the farm experience and his love of growing plants never faded. Plants, how they sprouted, how cuttings rooted, how trees were grafted, and how they grew and contributed to the eco-system, all became illustrations for his science classes. For Dick the quickest way to get him to try a new experiment was to say that it could not be done. So he built a 12' x 20' greenhouse, heated only by a wood burning stove, and began to raise pineapples and bananas in Northern California. The greenhouse also allowed him the opportunity to root less exotic azalea cuttings from plants in his own yard. Soon he had 4,000 to 5,000 plants needing new homes. Some he gave away, some he sold to local nurseries. Basically he was only interested in making enough money to support his hobby.

It was not until he retired that Dick really turned his attention to making his hobby a side line business to supplement his pension. Everything that he had always loved about growing plants was already there to enjoy, only the marketing presented him with a new challenge, for if you want to make money you cannot continue to give the plants away. Word of mouth advertising from old friends proved to be Dick's most effective sales tool and he found plenty of buyers for his plants. Once again back in touch with his farm roots, Dick says that he truly likes dealing with gardeners for he feels that he can always depend on people who are close to the soil.

A backyard nursery is also a good business for the retired person who never had any experience with plants, like our neighbor Sid Dunmore, who just wanted to keep active and make a little extra pocket money. For years his goats had wantonly eyed our field filled with tempting goodies, so it was with a sense of relief that we watched Sid fence off that portion of his field nearest ours and move his goats further away. Sid too had been watching our plants grow and decided he was going to raise plants on that section. Sid was 70, a retired police officer. He had never been involved with any aspect of the nursery industry, unless you count growing tomatoes in the garden. He asked my advice on what to grow, consulted other literature and collected grower catalogues. He finally decided on poplars and deodar cedars. He ordered the plants and had his handyman come in to help with the planting. Approaching it as an interesting and intriguing project, he set up his growing area to be relatively maintenance free with weed cloth on the ground and drip irrigation for the trees. I cannot say exactly what motivated Sid to raise a nursery crop, but it was clear that his rewards were almost immediate. As we sat sipping beer on his patio one summer afternoon he talked about how much pleasure he found watching those plants grow and how he wished he had done this while he was a younger man. A short time later, Sid learned he had cancer. This did not stop him from continuing on with his plants. In fact, instead of trying to liquidate everything, he simply got rid of the poplars and had his handyman return to help him transplant the cedars into larger containers. He really did just like watching the trees grow, taking both pride and pleasure in his enterprise. His widow has planted a small grove of cedars as his memorial.

Developing a nursery business in the backyard is something that can provide relaxation as well as profit for the mother who wants to stay at home to take care of young children. Such was the case with Rose who recounted to me how her interest in plants began at a very early age when she made an arrangement of the flowers her mother had given her while she sat in her highchair. By the time she was in the sixth grade she had so many African violets in every room of the house that her father built her a 7' x 18' lean-to hothouse adjacent to the garage. Rose even married into the plant business, finding a kindred spirit in a man whose parents owned a nursery. When her in-laws later sold their nursery, and her husband went into another business, Rose took out her own nursery license and grew bromeliads and other exotics in a 25' x 20' heated greenhouse in her backyard. The pleasure that Rose found in growing plants was soon put to another important purpose producing the extra money needed to send her daughter through private school. A decade of small scale growing for both pleasure and profit had passed when, following a sudden and unexpected divorce, Rose found herself a single parent and sole provider. She decided to expand her hobby into a full-time business. Although dealt a heavy blow by an unkind fate, Rose felt fortunate finding work she loved already there in the backyard. She picked up the pieces, propagated plants like crazy, and built a business, but more importantly for Rose, she was able to stay at home while she raised her daughter.

The backyard nursery is also the type of business that can be managed by a young person who wants to earn some extra money, but has no way to get to a job or no job to get. It can be a very good way for a teenager to earn the money to buy a truck and be able to write it off as a business deduction. Nor is the business beyond the capabilities of many people with physical or mental handicaps.

WHAT WILL IT TAKE TO START YOUR BACKYARD NURSERY?

Before you proceed with your plans for going into the nursery business, you must determine if your zoning allows this type of business to be operated from your home. If you are zoned for farm, commercial or industrial you should have little problem from the zoning department. Smaller residential lots are a different story. You can grow all the plants you want as a gardener, but business use of your property is more restricted. Many home occupation codes require that there be no exterior evidence of business activity. No outside storage of supplies, materials or products associated with the business may be permitted. All business activity may have to be confined within the house, garage or detached accessory structures. Enclosed agricultural accessory structures, such as greenhouses and shade houses, are generally allowed on residential property, but their size may be limited to 500 or 1,000 sq. ft. Even within such a small area, it is possible to generate several thousand dollars worth of plants a year. Check with your local planning and zoning department first before you apply for the required licenses. Tell them what you want to do and how you propose to do it and ask them for their help and suggestions in fulfilling your goals.

By deciding to operate a nursery in your backyard you have freed yourself from one of the major worries in starting a new business, finding a location. You need only determine what is possible with the space you already have, what tools and equipment are necessary, what supplies you must purchase and what types of plants to grow.

HOW MUCH SPACE DO YOU NEED?

How much space you need is a question relative to how much you want to earn and how much space your zoning allows you to use. Plants come in various sized containers which occupy a given space, but the amount of money that a space can generate will vary with the varieties of plants grown, their quality, the prevailing market conditions and the number of crops you can turn within a year. Let us consider first what is physically possible within a given area. Table 1.1 gives the area occupied by some standard nursery containers. Container sizes used to be given as gallon measurements, but in reality they do not hold the exact volume. Truth in advertising has led to simply describing the containers as a #1 or a #5 instead of a one gallon or a five gallon, which is a precise measurement of volume. In the trade vernacular the cans are still referred to by their gallon sizes and we will use the phrase throughout. If you calculate the math in Table 1.1, you see that the area for the cans is that of a square not of a circle. Although the can is round, the spaces between the curves are not used and the total space a can takes up on the ground is found by squaring its diameter. A square foot is 12" by 12" or 144 sq. in.. This means that you can get four #1 containers to a square foot, two #2s, one #5, and you need about two sq. ft. per #15 container.

In the small space of 100 sq. ft. you have room to accommodate 400 #1s, or 200 #2s, or 100 #5s, or about 50 #15s when placed can-to-can. If you space them further apart, you will have correspondingly fewer plants in the same space. If you are only interested in earning small amounts of extra spending cash, then a small area may be all that you need, but you probably have far more space available than 100 sq. ft., and those looking for more profit only need utilize more space. Just keep in mind that the more space you use for plants, the more additional space you will have to give to aisles between the rows.

Table 1.1 Container areas

Container type	Dimensions at top	Ground area needed
liner flat	17 " x 17 "	289 sq. in.
bedding flat	21 1/2" x 11"	237 sq. in.
#1	6" diameter	36 sq. in.
#2	8 1/2" diameter	72 sq. in.
#5	12" diameter	144 sq. in.
#15	16" diameter	256 sq. in.

Five gallon seedling maples rowed out can-to-can.

If you are limited to 1,000 sq. ft. in a covered accessory building, how do you maximize your space? Can-to-can is as close as you can get your spacing, but you need to be able to reach into the block of plants to pull weeds and maintain the plants, so you cannot put them in rows more than ten to thirteen gallon cans wide. I find twelve gallons a good row width, but a shorter person may prefer ten to a row. You need access on both sides of a six foot wide block of plants. Make your aisles about 2 1/2' to 3' wide. Let's say you are working with an area 40' long by 25' wide, confined by the walls of a structure. Place a five-can wide row of 6" diameter #1s along the whole length of the 40' wall, leave a 2 1/2' aisle, then put in a twelve-can row, leaving a 2 1/2' aisle on the long side, add another twelve-can row and another 2 1/2' aisle, and finish with another five-can row along the other wall. At the entrance on the 25' front wall allow a 2' side aisle in order to have access to the long aisles. Along the 25' back wall you can fill in the aisles with plants to a depth of five or six cans. This arrangement allows you to have about 2,700 gallon plants in a 1,000 sq. ft. area. Additional space can be utilized by placing hanging baskets over some of the aisles.

WHAT EQUIPMENT IS ESSENTIAL?

In your home nursery the tractors and the planting machines used by the large commercial operators can be replaced by the $15.00 square point shovel. I have used the same shovel for the last fifteen years, and although I have noticed lately that it does not do the same amount of work that it used to, it still appears to be very functional!

The electric carts and the tractor drawn flatbeds which the large nurseries use to transfer the plants into and out of the growing grounds can be replaced by the specially designed nursery handcart which is commonly used in the retail stores, or the mode of transportation can be as simple as a wagon or a wheelbarrow. Once the plants are moved to the growing grounds, the most important equipment for their maintenance is the water delivery system which can be a $6.00 hose.

Two additional inexpensive pieces of equipment are commonly used in plant production. Pruning shears are used both for making cuttings and for trimming and shaping plants. A good medium sized pair of shears useful for both purposes costs about $20.00. Sprayers are used to combat insect and weed problems. Two simple types are readily available and easy to use. In a tank sprayer, the spray must be mixed with water in the tank. Air is then put under pressure by pumping a hand operated plunger at the top of the sprayer. The spray is emitted through a nozzle which allows a great deal of control over where it is going. The second type, the hose-end sprayer, attaches to the hose and operates on water pressure. It is good for covering large areas or for spraying trees. Some types automatically proportion out the spray and mixing is unnecessary. It is a good idea to have separate sprayers for weed killers and insecticides.

Once the plant is grown and ready for sale, the time has come when you may need the largest piece of equipment, a delivery vehicle. Large wholesalers have fleets of semis, and in the spring when demand for plants is high you may have seen their trucks hauling two trailers. Inside those trailers metal brackets hold moveable wooden shelves. The plants are stacked on these shelves right to the top of the trailer. Thousands of plants are transported in one truckload. You do not need to be intimidated by this equipment because you do not need it.

The price of all wholesale plant material is listed in the catalogues as FOB point of origin. FOB is the abbreviation for "free on board." FOB point of origin means that the truck is loaded at no extra cost to the buyer, but the actual transportation charges to destination are extra. Most companies charge for delivery. Shipping is an extra overhead cost added to the list price of the plant material. Inability to deliver does not prevent you from entering the business. Many wholesalers have their customers come to the nursery to pick up their orders. The same options are available to you: either to deliver or to have the customers come to you, or both.

Let's discuss the options for those operations which will make deliveries. For smaller plants a van works well, but the most functional vehicle is the pickup truck. In a three-quarter ton pickup bed of standard size, you can fit just over 150 #1s or 55 #5s, and these numbers can be increased by stacking. This is done by leaving a slight space between the containers so that another row of plants can be placed on the rims of the two cans below and between the plants on either side. If well packed, the plants will not shift and damage can be avoided. The open bed of a pickup does not provide plants with protection against wind burn. For short distance hauling, wind burn can be minimized by driving at slower speeds. If you have to transport your plants a greater distance, you might consider a camper shell, but this also limits the number of tall plants that can be hauled since they must be laid down. Laying down plants in the open pickup bed also cuts down on wind burn and even fifteen gallon trees can be transported this way. Putting on side boards and tarping the plants will also cut down on transport damage. Having a pickup makes the whole business easier and the person who wants to do any substantial amount of business will find that a pickup becomes more and more a necessity, but not everyone has a truck to start with, so let's consider other options.

When I first started, I used my car for hauling supplies home and for delivering out plants. I sold to a nursery very near my house and I just made as many trips as necessary. This is not practical for someone who has to haul a large number of plants a longer distance. In this case a trailer is a very inexpensive option. If you are not yet in a position to own either a truck or a trailer, you can always consider renting something. Whatever you eventually use for delivery is an overhead expense and, therefore, tax deductible. This may be the perfect incentive to buy that truck. All or a portion of the cost of purchasing and operating the vehicle may be written off as a business expense against the profits from the plants. I only wish that I had thought of this when I was a teenager. I could have had a job at home suited to my own hours and earned the money for a set of wheels.

DO YOU NEED A CLIMATIZED GREENHOUSE?

A climate controlled greenhouse, the structure most commonly associated with a nursery business, provides an artificial climate within the area it encloses, maintaining temperatures within a certain range through the use of heaters when it is cold and cooling fans when it becomes too hot. Such climate control allows propagation of plants at any season of the year and maintains a safe climate for growing tender plants without worry of killing freezes. This all comes with a heavy price tag. Construction and operation costs vary depending on the size of the structure and the harshness of the climate. But before you even get to that point, construction of a greenhouse using gas and electricity requires a building permit and the city or county may choose to limit your options. If you already have a small greenhouse which you are using for your hobby, you have a valuable tool for profitable plant production. For the many more of you who prefer not to go to the expense of a greenhouse, rest assured that a climate controlled greenhouse is not a necessity for the backyard grower. For those unwilling to be fettered by the constraints of weather, there are inexpensive ways to create artificial micro-climates. Let's consider some of the other options.

COLD FRAMES

A main concern of the nurseryman is the cold. Cold prevents seed germination, cold restricts growth and cold can kill. The natural source of heat is the sun. The walls and roof of the greenhouse allow the rays of the sun to pass through a covering of fiberglass, thus heating the air trapped inside. This principle also applies to any frame covered with glass or plastic. One such structure called a cold frame, because it has no artificial source of heat, is simple to construct. Nail four lengths of 2"x 8" or 2"x 12" boards into a rectangular or square frame to create the four walls of a box. The ground is the bottom of the box. Use flats for holding the media and plants. Make the back wall slightly higher by adding an extra piece of wood and put two tapered boards on the sides to create a slope toward the front of the box. Create a separate top for the box by stretching clear plastic over a frame of 1" x 1" strips of wood. Attach to the back wall with hinges so that it can be opened and closed readily. The reason for this is twofold: first, without fans to draw off the excess heat, cold frames can become too hot for the plants inside; secondly, the plants must be watered, since the plastic covering eliminates any benefits of rain.

The heat stored by the plastic promotes seed germination and rooting of cuttings, but the heat cannot be maintained when there is no sun and when extremely cold temperatures dominate. Cold frames have their limitations, but they do provide free heat during the colder seasons of the year and expand the growing season.

PLASTIC HOUSES

A plastic house, which is a large frame covered by plastic sheeting, is simply a cold frame on a larger scale. A common type looks like a Quonset hut. It is usually high enough for a person to walk down the center, with the height decreasing out toward the sides. The low sides accommodate bedding flats perfectly since they do not need height. The top covering is tightly fastened and cannot be opened. Heat does not build up as quickly as in a cold frame because there is much more air to heat. When there is too much heat, both ends are opened up to create ventilation. You can devise any frame from wood, plastic PVC pipe or aluminum, but be sure to give some pitch or curve to the roof to allow for rain runoff. If wind is not a worry, you can stretch the plastic over the frame and simply anchor it along the sides by using rocks or soil.

INSULATION FABRICS

There are a number of different fabrics on the market designed to insulate plants against frost and freeze damage. In colder climates, foam insulation blankets are fastened on frames in order to protect containerized material from freezing. In milder climates growers use a polypropylene fabric as a crop cover. The fabric is so thin and light it can be placed directly on the plants. It can be left on the plants for long periods since it is porous to air, light and water, and it is so light that even seedlings lift it as they grow. Frost protection with different fabrics goes down to 24° F. The wholesale price for a 1725 sq.ft. roll of 1/2 oz./yd. fabric which transmits 85% sunlight and protects down to 28° F is about $50.00.

Rolls of insulation blanket spread over Quonset type frame for winter protection of container material.

A UNIQUE APPROACH

Each nurseryman creates a business which is unique to that individual, developed and nurtured from one's own conceptions and experience. One of the more unusual operations is All

21

Seasons Nursery run by Ron Motz and Janet Bozzo on three leased acres in Elk Grove, California. On a visit to the nursery one is immediately struck by the virtual absence of one gallon container stock. In place of these common nursery pots are numerous plastic crates filled with blue cylinders sticking up over the top of the crates. Ron and Janet have developed a simple procedure to grow and transplant seedlings with virtually no disruption to the root systems. They seed directly into open-ended cylinders of blue tinted polyester film which are placed on a sheet of newspaper in meshed open-bottomed crates. The crates are raised off the ground, so that when the roots of the plants reach the bottom of the cylinder, they cease to grow downward and spread laterally. This is a process called air pruning. Without waiting for the roots to fill the whole cylinder, they transplant the tender seedlings into five gallon containers, mylar cylinder and all. The soil is firmed in around the cylinder, which is then removed. The roots are never disturbed, so there is no transplant shock or slowdown in the growth process. Moreover, they have found that if they do not remove the cylinder, but only pull it up a bit higher on the plant, it provides a greenhouse effect for the seedling in the cooler weather, adding as much as five to fifteen degrees of extra warmth right around the plant. Each cylinder then functions as a low-tech mini greenhouse.

This unique process was developed in Ron's backyard in a slightly round-a-bout way. In 1976 Ron went into the business of reclaiming silver from X-ray film and soon found that he had tons of mylar left over which he had to haul to the dump. Convinced that there must be something better to do with it, he recalled seeing how the California Department of Forestry had used open-end sleeve technology in producing their seedlings. As a boy living on the family farm in Lodi, he had used similar methods propagating pistachio trees in tar-paper sleeves. The flexible mylar was easily converted into such an open-end sleeve by rolling and stapling. Soon Ron had 25,000 eucalyptus seedlings growing in his mylar sleeves. Open-end sleeves were nothing new, but mylar was, and in the course of recycling a waste product, Ron found that this type of plastic created a special climate which produced rapid growth not realized in the traditional sleeves. His method has come to the attention of university environmental horticulture experts and has been cited in journal articles. Ron and Janet continue to improve on the process, and now besides growing and selling plants, they are marketing their trademarked Blue-X shelters.

SHADE CLOTH

Freezing temperatures and frost are not the only weather concerns of growers. Excessive summer sun and heat are detrimental to many nursery crops. Shade cloth is a woven or knitted polypropylene fabric which protects plants from the sun by absorbing all light except what passes directly through its tiny porous holes. Black shade cloth absorbs heat and re-radiates it to the growing area; green shade cloth absorbs less heat. Shade-loving plants require the micro-climate created by shade cloth. It is also beneficial to bedding material or liner stock in small containers which dry quickly on very hot days and can burn without protection. In the hottest climates it helps keep the containers cooler and spares the roots the extremely hot temperatures which black plastic containers can generate. Shade cloth is rated by the percentage of sunlight it screens out. Some types and prices are given in Table 1.2.

Table 1.2 Shade cloth

Shade percentage%	price per sq.ft.	widths
30%	$.09	6',10',12'
47%	$.09	6',10',12'
63%	$.10	6',10',12'
80%	$.14	6',10',12'
85%	$.18	6',10',12'
95%	$.25	6',10',12'

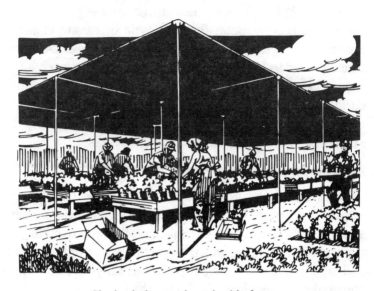

Shade cloth on pole and cable frame.

It is possible to use the same frame for plastic or shade cloth, exchanging one for the other in different seasons. If you intend to use only shade cloth, the frame does not need any pitch or curve at the top like the frames covered with plastic because rain passes through the cloth. Since the cloth's purpose is to screen out light, it is frequently used only as a top covering. However, one can enclose the sides of the frame as well, creating a shade house. This not only filters out light from all angles, but also creates a different micro-climate which in winter offers some frost protection and in summer retains humidity.

WHAT LICENSES ARE NECESSARY?

You do not need a license to begin growing plants. If you are inexperienced in plant production and are unsure of your abilities, you do not need to spend money to obtain a license in order to find out if you have a green thumb. License laws regulate plants offered for sale, but until you are ready to offer plants for sale, you are only a gardener or hobbyist. When you decide to sell your plants, there are three basic things you have to consider: the nursery license, the business license, and the seller's permit.

NURSERY LICENSE

It is unlawful to sell plants without an annual nursery license. Nurseries are agricultural businesses controlled by the departments of food and agriculture in the various states. Generally the license fee is paid to the state and the license is issued by the state, but enforcement and inspections are done by the county agriculture commissions. Application forms for the license can be obtained from either the county or the state and you should find the telephone number under the government listings for Department of Agriculture or Department of Food and Agriculture for your county. They will answer your questions on licensing requirements and procedures and will send you the necessary forms.

However, if you are just beginning to consider turning your hobby into a business, you may not even need to pay a fee for your license. For example, California allows the hobbyist to have a fee exempt license if the following conditions are met: 1) annual sales must be under $500, 2) the applicant must report to the Commissioner of his county his intention to sell plants, 3) all the plants must be of one's own production and 4) applicant must sell the plants for planting in the county in which they were produced.

In our case, California charges a fee of $100 for the nursery license. This fee is for nurseries under one acre; the fee increases as the acreage increases. The fee goes to offset the cost of a yearly inspection of the nursery by a county agriculture inspector. The more area to be inspected, the more it costs for the license. The agriculture inspection serves to identify any problems with insects or plant diseases potentially harmful to the industry as a whole if allowed to spread. If a problem is detected in your nursery, the affected plants will be tagged with a non-compliance warning tag and sale of the tagged items will be prohibited until the problem is corrected and the tag is removed on a follow-up inspection. This is not really a stigma on you or your nursery, just a problem that needs correction, usually by spraying the affected plants or removing the offending weeds, and usually all is fine within two weeks to a month.

Besides inspections there are a series of regulations and restrictions which apply on the state level. Sometimes certain plants cannot be grown or sold in certain areas, or if grown in one area they cannot be shipped into another. There are times when special quarantine areas are set up and further restrictions will apply. For the small grower most of these things will not be a problem. You have a wide choice of what to grow; simply avoid the problem plants.

BUSINESS LICENSE
In some cases, if you have the nursery license and an agricultural zoning, you may not need a business license; but the probability is that you will need a business license. This license is issued by the county or city, and different local governments have different regulations. For the specific restrictions and fees, contact the government agency which has jurisdiction over your area.

The most common restrictions placed on a home business are the following: 1) no outside storage or display of material or product, 2) no customer traffic is allowed to the house, 3) no business signs are permitted, 4) deliveries are limited to a few times a month, 5) hazardous chemicals are prohibited and 6) restrictions are placed on hiring any help. Even so, you will find that you can operate successfully within these parameters. If you stretch your parameters too far and generate neighborhood complaints over the way you are operating your business, you may find your license revoked. Be a considerate neighbor, your business depends on it.

FICTITIOUS BUSINESS NAME

You can operate your business under your own name or you can use your surname in your business name with no additional legal requirements. But if you decide to call your business something else like Green Acres Nursery, you will have to file an application for a fictitious business name. This simply puts on public record the names of the owners of a business operating under a fictitious business name. Generally the forms are obtained from and filed with the county recorder or with the office where you obtain your business license. Publication of a notice of a fictitious business name must be made in a local newspaper.

If you operate your business under your own name, any checks you accept can be deposited into your personal account at your bank; however, having a fictitious business name, or even having the word "Nursery" added behind your name, will compel you to have a business account at your bank in order to negotiate those checks. Business accounts are more expensive to maintain than personal, but they can also offer you the opportunity of accepting credit cards.

SELLER'S PERMIT

If you sell taxable merchandise or provide a taxable service, you must also have a Seller's Permit issued by the state. There is usually no fee for this permit since what it really does is make you an authorized tax collecting agent for the state. In some cases deposits may be required. Besides giving you the responsibility for collecting the sales tax, the Seller's Permit also allows you to enjoy an exemption from paying the sales tax on supplies which actually become part of your product. This means that you may be able to buy your soil and containers and even fertilizer without having to pay the sales tax. You can also purchase plants or supplies for resale without paying sales tax, and hence the Seller's Permit is frequently referred to as a Resale Number. When any plant finally sells to the customer who will take it home and use it, the sales tax is levied.

If you sell it to the end user, you are responsible for collecting the sales tax. If you are selling to retailers, they can use their permit to buy from you tax free, and they become the ones responsible for collecting the sales tax when they sell to their customers. To prove that it is not your responsibility to collect the sales tax, you must get a resale certificate from your customer. This is a simple form available from stationary stores for about $.10. Your customer provides his resale number and certifies that the product will be resold by him in the form of tangible property and that he will pay the appropriate sales tax. You will be asked to certify the same when you use your permit.

You need a Seller's Permit no matter who you sell to, even if you never intend to sell directly to the end user, and you will have to file a tax return even if there is no money due. Sales tax forms, like income tax forms, are subject to audit and this brings up the topic of record keeping.

RECORD KEEPING AND TAXES

You have to keep records of your sales and your expenses on paper, not in your head. Keeping a record of income is as simple as noting the date of a transaction with the dollar amount of the sale.

Tax forms treat income under several different categories. For example, California sales tax forms make the main distinction between wholesale (non-taxable) and retail (taxable) sales and there are sub-categories for other tax exempt sales: the sale of annual vegetable plants is considered non-taxable food sales and a planting fee is considered non-taxable labor, while a delivery fee is taxable. If you set up your books so that your entries of expenses and income coincide with categories on your state's tax forms, you will save yourself a great deal of trouble when it comes time to fill out these forms.

The IRS considers income from growing plants to be farm income and it is reported on Schedule F. This form is divided into two parts: the first concerns the portion of your farm income produced from products that you simply bought and resold, the second deals with your own production and the specific expenses incurred in growing your material. It is difficult to sort this all out at the end of the year if you only have the two categories of income and outgo, so set up separate categories for these different types of sales. If two-thirds of your gross income is generated by your production of plant material, you are considered a farmer and you have two payment options. You may pay an estimated tax by January 15 and any remainder by April 15 when you file your return, or you must file and pay the full amount by March 1. If your gross farm income is less than two-thirds of your total income, you must pay quarterly. Request IRS Publication 225.

If your nursery income is chiefly from reselling, not growing, you may need to file a Schedule C instead of Schedule F and pay quarterly to avoid penalties. In addition to paying federal income tax, self-employed business people must pay self-employment tax. This is your social security tax. However, since you are your own employer, you must pay not only the employee portion, but also the employer portion of the tax. In 1996 this was 15.3% of your income after business deductions. This overview is not intended as tax advice. For specific tax advice on your situation consult a tax advisor.

INSURANCE

Gardening and growing plants is a relatively safe activity, but in turning it into a business you have to take into consideration your increased liability risks. A homeowner policy is not going to cover your business. If your zoning allows customers to come to your home, look into liability insurance. The best rates for liability insurance will probably be found through membership in your state nurserymen association.

If you do not have customers to your home, your exposure to the public is quite limited, but in transporting the plants to market your liability increases, Your auto insurer may want to raise your insurance rates and change your coverage to cover the business usage of your vehicle. Discuss costs and risks with your agent in order to find what is best for you.

NURSERYMEN ASSOCIATIONS

Membership in nursery associations is voluntary. Associations offer their members a number of events and benefits. They sponsor trade shows and garden shows, publish directories of their members, some publish magazines and buyers guides for wholesale materials. They also have group health, property and casualty insurance plans. Meetings of the local chapters offer opportunities to meet and socialize with other people in the industry and opportunities to do business. Annual conventions bring members together from throughout the state. The small size of your nursery does not prevent you from joining the association. A list of associations is in Appendix One.

CHAPTER 2

GETTING STARTED

HOW DO YOU DETERMINE WHAT TO GROW?
Since climate places limitations on the types of plants that can grow in your particular location, it is a primary consideration in making your decisions about what to grow. The United States Department of Agriculture has divided the country into zones of plant hardiness as shown in the map on page 32. Most garden books refer to these zones in discussing what grows where, and many wholesale nursery catalogues refer to plant hardiness with these zone numbers. For western gardeners, *The Sunset Western Garden Book* divides the climates of the eleven western states into twenty-four sub-climates. Sunset's plant listings give the zone numbers in which the species and variety grow. These maps and zonings give the hardiness for plants in the ground and help you determine what types of plants customers want in a certain area, but they are not a guide to what will survive the winter cold in containers. The ground provides extra insulation for a plant's root system, but containerized material is more exposed and fragile. The containers can and do freeze solid. Serious root damage is possible, and for many plants, any extended time in the frozen container can be fatal. Additional protection is necessary in many areas in order to get containerized material through the winter. However, knowledge of a plant's cold hardiness is valuable information because

USDA PLANT HARDINESS ZONE MAP

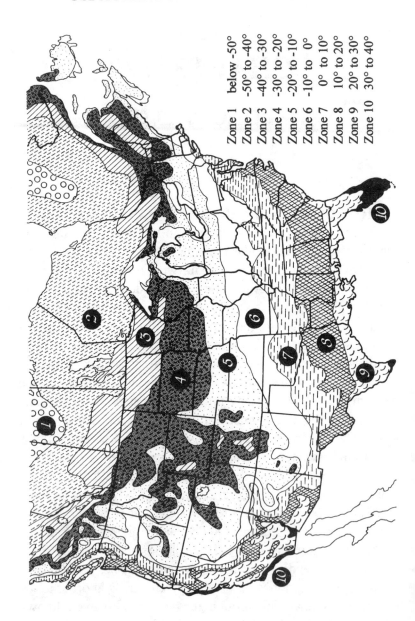

Zone 1	below -50°
Zone 2	-50° to -40°
Zone 3	-40° to -30°
Zone 4	-30° to -20°
Zone 5	-20° to -10°
Zone 6	-10° to 0°
Zone 7	0° to 10°
Zone 8	10° to 20°
Zone 9	20° to 30°
Zone 10	30° to 40°

you can expect a containerized plant suited to zone two or three to be more tolerant of freezing temperatures than plants suited to zone seven or eight.

Moreover, in giving you only cold hardiness, the USDA zone map does not tell you that many of those plants that are cold hardy in sub-zero temperatures are not suited to the hot summer temperatures of the southern zones. Lilacs, for example, need cold winter temperatures in order to bloom, and fruit trees need a certain number of winter chill hours in order to bear fruit. Although the plants will live in warmer climates, they cannot meet the customer's expectations.

To grow what one likes is perhaps the most logical choice for a gardener turned nurseryman. There are certain advantages in doing this. Besides continuing to enjoy the pleasures that raising these plants has given you, you already have experience in growing these particular plants and a familiarity with their habits, their cycles and their needs in the different seasons. This knowledge is important because in any wholesale nursery operation there are two distinctly different aspects to the business: that of growing the plants and that of selling the plants. You can never achieve any level of success in the second without expertise in the first. For those who have proven to themselves their ability to grow particular plants, the prospects of selling those plants is the only thing to be tested.

If you make the assumption that because you like certain plants, everyone else likes them as well, you may be very surprised. We have learned, to our profit, that you do not have to like everything that you grow and sell. Before you make your decision about what to grow, you may want to look into the diverse numbers of plants which have an established and dependable marketability. This is of greatest importance for those who have little or no experience with plants, but are induced by the profit potential to try a backyard nursery.

Without a background in the nursery business, how do you determine which plants sell well? You can always ask a grower, but if you were successfully growing certain types of plants without excessive competition, would you tell someone to grow the same plants and become your competitor? The retailer is the best place to gather your information. Any retailer can count off ten plants which sell year after year in the different categories of bedding, flowering perennials, shrubs, vines and trees. Whatever information you may gather by asking questions can be supplemented by your own observations. Tour the local retail nurseries to see what kinds of plants they carry. You do not need to stand around watching what people buy, just walk around and note how much space in the beds has been given to the various plants. Those plants which have been given more space are usually the more popular ones.

Someone is buying the plants you see in the nurseries and is planting them in the landscape. As you travel around in your own area you can note what types of landscaping plants appear most frequently around the newer homes, office complexes and shopping centers. Look to the newer areas to see what is currently favored. Plants change in popularity and some of the plants widely used years ago are seldom used today. If you do not know the names of some plants, cut a piece with leaves or flowers and take it to a nursery for identification.

Another way to learn what sells is to start reading the advertisements in the newspaper. You will note that the most heavily advertised plants are the bedding flowers and small blooming plants. Sold at cost or even as loss leaders, these plants get people to come into the nursery and they are chosen for advertising because there is a good demand for them. Bedding plants as a group are referred to as "color" and are the mainstay of the retail nursery. Their success points out one simple rule to keep in mind when growing plants: flowers sell the plant. This rule applies to anything that blooms, including trees and shrubs and vines, and the season they are in bloom is their prime selling time.

SO, IF IN DOUBT ABOUT WHAT TO GROW, GROW SOMETHING THAT FLOWERS.

It is also worthwhile to read popular gardening magazines. Readers go to retail nurseries specifically looking for the plants featured in the articles. Note what types of plants are being recommended. For example, drought tolerant plants may be the current focus and the retailers need a selection of different types of such plants in order to satisfy the demand created by the magazine articles.

Once you have some plants in mind, you can ask more specific questions and clarify the market potential. There are several things you must know and most of the information can be obtained from your local retail nurseryman who can give you a general impression of the market.

You should first ask if the nursery stocks the plants which you want to grow. Is there a demand for the plants? Can they give you an idea how many they sell in a season or in a year? You will find that certain nurseries promote some plants more heavily than others. Your best understanding of the market will be achieved if you talk to people at a number of different nurseries in your area. If a nursery does not carry a plant you are interested in growing, ask if it is because there is no market for that type of plant, or because there is no source for the plant. This can be a tricky question because there may be no market because there is no supply or no supply because there is no market. There are also specialized areas in which retailers have no experience, so you may also want to talk to landscapers and landscape architects.

If the plants that you want to grow are sold at the nursery, take a look at them in order to better assess your competition. Consider three areas: quality, price and service. You can inspect the plants at the retail nursery to determine the quality; you can check catalogues or price lists for the pricing. The retailers may tell you what they are currently paying. Simply ask. You will have to inquire directly of the retailers whether they are happy with their level of service and what concessions the supplier may have made to them. For example, if a supplier services the bedding tables and replaces the dead or unmarketable material, you may not even want to try to compete for that market, but rather turn your attention either to other plants or other markets.

Once you know what price you can get for the plants, you need to know what it will cost you to produce them. In other words, the larger market sets the price and what it costs you to produce your material has no bearing on what you can charge for it, unless you are the only one growing the plant. The following chapters break down the cost factors for plants in various sized containers. This will help you calculate your fixed costs for materials. There are some costs which are variable such as water and utilities, especially if you are using a well or a greenhouse.

SPECIALIZATION AND NICHE MARKETING

The purpose of your research is to obtain knowledge about the feasibility of selling certain types of plants so that you can better focus your efforts on what will be successful for you. No matter how saturated the market may appear, there is always some small niche that is not being exploited. For many small growers, identifying a niche overlooked or simply not serviced by others has proven to be a dependable and profitable business. A niche does not need to be exotic. You may find that the market is filled with house plants in six-inch containers, but there is virtually nothing available in two-inch pots. There may be a wide variety of vegetable starter plants available, but no one may have taken into consideration the ethnic market for certain types of vegetables, or the ever increasing market for organic or heirloom vegetables and herbs. There are niches for rare varieties or species. Sometimes the niche is to be found even in common species already widely grown by many other nurseries, for by growing a high quality plant and selling it at a price sufficiently below the competition, you may carve out a niche and virtually control your local market.

Specializing is the best way to create your own niche in the marketplace and it has several advantages. You can get to know everything there is to know about your particular types of plants. For some growers this has meant that they have become the recognized experts in their area, and as their reputation has increased so has their business. By nature then, a specialty nursery is the type of business that tends to start slowly and build steadily.

Specializing has great advantages in the production end of the business. Once you have found what works, continue to trust the process. However, specialization does have its limitations when it comes to the marketing end of the business. You have to take into consideration the nature of your local market, asking how much of your crop it can absorb. If the crop is small enough there may be no problem, but the more you produce of one type of plant the greater the distribution area you will require in order to sell the plant. If you want your business to continue to expand, you will have to ask yourself how far you are willing to ship your material in order to get it sold. The large growers ship their plants nationwide, yet even they find that from time to time they have overproduced some species and the market cannot absorb the supply.

DIVERSIFICATION

Diversification will increase your customer base. Whether you are dealing directly with the public or wholesaling to a retail nursery, the more choices you offer, the more chances you have to sell something. There is also less need to expand your market area, since by expanding your customers' options you increase your market potential within the same area. You should not try to be all things to all people because you will find that your expertise will not extend to everything that grows. Even with diversification you will have to limit the number of things that you grow, narrowing your inventory to what you grow well and what you can market at a reasonable profit.

SEASONAL VERSUS YEAR-ROUND

Another question you must ask yourself is whether you want to operate your business on a year-round or seasonal basis. Many retail nursery operations do not remain open for the winter where the climate is too harsh or the level of buying activity is not sufficient to justify the overhead. This is not difficult for the retailer who is simply handling a product. Seasonal marketing, however, requires more planning for the grower who must invest time in creating the product. If you intend to market any product in a single season, there is additional market research that you must do. 1) Know the growing requirements of the particular plants you intend to grow. How long does it take to get from stage A to stage B? 2) When is the prime market season for the plant? Your target date and how long it takes to get there tell you when you have to start. 3) Does the plant need special conditions to meet these requirements? Climate will present the greatest limitations on these seasonal requirements.

In many areas, cold weather brings an end to both plant growth and plant sales. Artificial climates and insulation fabrics will help the hardier plants winter over, but without adequate protection, container growing in the colder climates is best treated as a seasonal business operated during the growing season. Without a greenhouse in these harsh climates your choices of what to grow become more limited, but there are a number of strategies offered in the next five chapters which a backyard grower can use for container growing in the colder climates.

In the warmer zones, nursery business is conducted year-round and in some zones, the evergreen plants grow all twelve months of the year. However, even if year-round growing and selling is possible, you must still ask yourself if you want to operate year-round or on a seasonal basis. Quite simply you may not want to take care of plants all year, but rather raise a six month crop, sell it and spend the money on a vacation.

FINDING SOURCES FOR SUPPLIES

When you have determined what to grow, how do you find the supplies necessary to produce it? There are four basic things you need: containers, soil, fertilizer and labels. A great deal of television, newspaper and magazine advertising is aimed at gardeners, telling them where to find plants and supplies in the retail trade, but how does the gardener turned nurseryman go about finding the wholesale suppliers who are selling to the growers producing the plants? For your convenience, a number of distributors have been listed in Appendix Two. The suppliers' names and addresses come from lists provided by fertilizer and container manufacturers. This offers you a good place to start, but it is by no means exhaustive, nor is it intended to be. When you find a distributor, you have found a source for most of what you need: containers, media, fertilizer, chemicals, coverings and even structures. Some even broker plant material. Minimum orders are required by distributors ranging from as little as $100 to $250. Prices are FOB point of origin and fertilizers and planting media cannot be shipped UPS.

If you are looking for a specific product and you have not found the distributor who carries it, copy down the manufacturer's name and address which is usually printed on the package or label. The plastic nursery pots usually have the manufacturer's name and city on the bottom. We found some containers stamped with a toll free phone number. If street addresses are incomplete and phone numbers are not given, simply call information for the city in which the manufacturer is located and obtain the phone number. Most manufacturers will not sell to you directly, since they use distributors, but any manufacturer will be happy to tell you where to find the nearest distributor.

CONTAINERS

Containers are plant packaging. There is tremendous variation in the types and sizes of plant containers. Distributors carry a full line to meet your needs. Containers are sold by case units and can be shipped UPS. Different types will be discussed in greater detail in each stage of production.

Unlike other packaging, nursery containers can be reused when the product is removed since the container is usually not damaged in the removal of the plant. This creates a recycle market for used containers, but you have to go out and find it yourself. Where do you look?

Various types of plastic nursery containers.

The best sources for large numbers of used containers are landscape contractors. They install thousands of plants and must remove the empty containers from the job sites. Your best opportunity to obtain the containers is to watch the activity on new construction sites in your area. When you see landscape crews beginning to install plant material, stop at the site and find the foreman. Ask if they have a use for the empty containers or if they will be throwing them away. This blatant attempt to get them for free sometimes works. We have come across landscape contractors who have traveled to the site from a great distance and know no ready place to sell the containers locally. They have no intention of hauling them home, and they need to get rid of them to clean up the site in order to meet their contract terms. They may be happy to have you participate in the clean up by collecting the containers and hauling them off for free. This will not happen often.

Most contractors know someone who will pay for the containers. They may return them to the nursery for credit, and sometimes they may have paid a deposit on the containers. However, unless they have a special relationship with the plant supplier, it usually makes no difference to them who buys the containers. It might as well be you standing there with money in hand. In fact, they are happier to take cash rather than receive a credit on future purchases from a nursery.

If you fail to find containers on job sites, this does not mean that they have already been sold. Usually the local landscaper hauls the containers back to his own storage yard where they sit until he gets around to contacting a nursery. If you contact him first, the containers can probably be yours. The landscaper listings in the Yellow Pages offer a lengthy list of potential sources of containers.

Worry over potential disease contamination from containers purchased from landscape contractors is not a real concern, since they are planting healthy material on the job sites. Retail nurseries are a source for used containers which may be more suspect, because some of the containers may have come from plants which died and were dumped. Problems may be lurking in the residual soil. But just as many plants are dumped because they are unmarketable, not dead; and sometimes customers who do not have the heart to throw the empty cans in the garbage bring them back to the retail store. In our experience we have found little reason to worry about contamination, but if you are in a climate where fungus diseases are easily transmitted, it is better to be careful about a nursery source or be prepared to sterilize containers.

SOIL

Where do you get the soil for your containers? Your backyard is probably not the best source, unless your soil is very good and your goal is to eventually hand dig a swimming pool. So you are stuck paying real money for dirt. Most gardeners are familiar with bagged planting soils. You can find respected brand name planting mixes priced at $2.50 retail for a one cu. ft. bag, which translates to $67.50 per cu. yd. This price is actually less than the wholesale price of some commercial potting soils sold to growers. The special grower soils are blends of sphagnum peat moss, perlite, gypsum, and dolomite lime. The wholesale price for a compressed four cu. ft. bale which yields approximately seven and one-half cu. ft. of mix is about $23.00. That is about $84.00 a cu. yd. The cost is high because these commercial mixes contain a higher percentage of peat moss which is the most expensive ingredient in planting mix.

Commercial planting mixes are used mainly for seed and cutting propagation, bedding and vegetable starts, house plants and hanging baskets. You can cut costs by waiting for sales or by asking for quantity discounts on ten bags or more. The deepest discount can be found by buying broken bags. Small tears are simply taped, but badly torn bags or bags whose plastic has split or deteriorated from the hot sun are unmarketable and a nuisance at stores which do not plant their own material. If larger amounts of soil are needed, the best prices on bagged soils can be obtained by buying wholesale in pallet quantities, generally forty to sixty bags a pallet. The price drops closer to $40.00 per cu. yd. However, delivery requires a semi and a fork lift, which may not be permitted by the restrictions of your licensing for a home business.

If you only need small quantities for propagation or for a few special plants, it is easiest to buy bagged planting mix at retail prices, but bagged soil is too expensive to use for general container planting. Greater cost savings are found if you mix your own soil, but there is no point in trying to reproduce the exact formula of the bagged mixes for there will be no significant savings in buying the components separately. Two suitable mixes were developed years ago by the University of California at Los Angeles and the John Innes Horticultural Institution in England which used three basic, readily available components: loam or topsoil, peat moss and sand. The Innes formula blended them in the following proportions.

seedling mix:	general potting mix
2 parts loam	7 parts loam
1 part peat moss	3 parts peat moss
1 part sand	2 parts sand

Peat moss has become rather expensive, so to save money you must reduce the amount of peat moss or substitute another component. Peat moss is seldom used in field grown container crops today, unless they are acid loving. Compost is the component which replaces peat moss. Compost is decomposed organic material and it can be made from a wide variety of materials, including leaves, wood chips, sawdust and grass. One of the benefits of using compost is its disease controlling properties. It contains beneficial organisms that are antagonistic to disease-causing organisms which attack roots. Three naturally occurring fungicides which help control soil-borne diseases have been identified in compost.

Compost, topsoil and sand are available in bags. The retail price of topsoil and compost is about $2.00 per cu. ft. This is still almost as expensive as the mixed potting soil. The price of a 100 lb. bag of sand is about $4.00. However, all three of these components, unlike peat moss, can be purchased in bulk quantities.

Bulk soils are found at some retail nurseries and at landscape supply and rock yards. In some areas compost can be purchased cheaply from cities which make it from the curb side pick up of yard trimmings or from electric utilities which make it from tree trimmings. Bulk soils are usually priced by the cubic yard or half-yard. Prices differ between suppliers, but a workable figure for topsoil or loam is about $18.00/yd., compost is also about $18.00/yd. and course sand is about $28.00/yd. Discounts are frequently available on ten yard loads or you might receive a nursery discount of 10% even on smaller amounts. You should always ask if discounts are available because they usually are.

Soils can be picked up at the supplier's yard or delivered. Only about one yard of the heavier materials can be carried by a pickup. Delivery charges usually apply for orders under five or six yards, but the larger amounts are delivered free within a local area. Delivery to your home business should not create a problem with your license restrictions because these landscape materials are delivered to neighborhoods all the time. However, storage may be a problem and you should have a space available where the soil can be dumped behind the fence line. You do not want a large pile of soil on your driveway creating an eyesore for your neighbors. Also keep in mind that loaded dump trucks are very heavy and can crack concrete driveways.

When dealing with bulk soils, one truth will soon become evident to you. Not all soils are created equal. Some suppliers mix topsoil, sand and compost together and call it a planting mix or a nursery mix. Consider these mixes first, but do not think that just because a bulk supplier calls a blended soil planting mix that it is what you need. Do not order sight unseen. Go to the different bulk yards, examine handfuls of the blended soils and then examine the components separately. Look closely at the topsoil and compost. When I started, I found the topsoil quite heavy. I could see many grains of sand in it and I quickly concluded that the topsoil already had enough sand. More sand would only have made the soil mix heavier and people do not like to carry heavy cans. I wanted a lighter and looser mix. Compost is the organic material which is used to lighten soil mixes, but it too varies in composition and weight. I simply chose the lightest compost. Let us note here that you want compost light in weight, not light in color. Well-made compost is usually brown or black in color. Lighter color indicates that the compost is fresh and still in the process of decomposing. The microorganisms which break down the organic material are themselves using nitrogen and they will rob it from other sources if they cannot get enough from the compost. Young compost essentially eats up the plant's food.

An easy way to mix soil is to measure it out by the shovelful, throwing it into a pile on the ground. The ratios you actually use need not be hard and fast since the textures of the components will vary with the source. What you are looking for in the end product is loose soil with good aeration and drainage, yet a soil which can retain enough water for growth. Its ability to hold water makes peat moss particularly useful in flats and small pots which have a tendency to dry out quickly. If you use peat moss, which is highly acidic, you should also add lime in order to lower the soil acidity for non-acid loving plants. Also add your fertilizer to the soil before you mix. Then simply turn the mixture over several times with your shovel. If the components of your soil are very dry when you begin to mix them together, especially if you use peat moss, moisten the soil to cut down on the dust.

Once I found what I liked, I just continued to order the same thing. For years, I mixed the topsoil and compost in ratios which looked good to me and added my fertilizer to the mix. If I needed even lighter mixes for propagation, I simply added perlite. But over the years I noticed that each time I got a new load of soil, the compost kept getting heavier. I cut down on the amount of topsoil I was using and increased the compost. Soon, what I was buying as compost seemed to contain such a high percentage of mineral soil that I decided to try the compost alone. It worked just fine and there was no more mixing. This was wonderful! It points out two thing you should keep in mind. First, the quality of the material will vary as sources change; and secondly, you can save yourself a great deal of labor if you can find a soil which you can use without mixing. In all probability, that soil will not be topsoil, but consider the mixed soils, and the soils which the landscape supply yards label as compost, mulch or humus. Remember, what you need is good aeration and drainage with enough water retention to promote growth. Almost any medium which satisfies these requirements will work. Nutrients need play no role whatsoever in your choice of soil. Pay no attention to a supplier's claim that a soil has been fortified with nitrogen or trace elements; what little nutrient value these soils contain will quickly leach out with watering. The fertilizer which you add yourself will take care of the plant's food needs.

Worry mainly about drainage. Put the soil to a test before you buy any large quantity. What's the test? Obtain a sample, a single gallon can of soil will do. Leave about two inches of space at the top of the can and add water. Watch how it is absorbed. It should soak in fairly quickly and not sit on the surface. It will take several waterings before a dry soil is saturated. Once you are sure the soil is completely wet, lift the can to see how heavy it is. A very heavy can indicates that the soil retains too much water. Dump the soil out. Ideally it should break apart in your hand. If it sticks together like clay, do not use it.

By the same token, try to avoid a medium which drains so quickly that it retains no moisture. A portion of mineral soil mixed with the organic material helps maintain moisture. In some commercial mixes which contain no mineral elements, polymers have been added to the media. These are superabsorbent crystals designed to soak up water and hold it as a reservoir for the plant, releasing it back into the soil as it is needed. Polymers can extend the time between waterings and are very beneficial where water is expensive. Polymers themselves are expensive with prices between $200.00 and $300.00 for a 50 lb. bag. However, since only small amounts are necessary per plant, it is worth considering for the savings both in water and in labor.

Once you have found bulk soils you think will meet your needs, there is one more test you should make before investing in a truckload. This test is for weeds. While the bagged soils are sterilized to kill weed seeds that may be lurking in the mix, bulk soils are not so treated. A simple test for weeds is to put the soil in a flat and water it. Weeds grow quickly and in seven to ten days you should see any unwanted crop sprouting.

FERTILIZER
Quite simply, fertilizer is plant food. A plant will not grow without the three basic elements of nitrogen, phosphorus and potassium. Manufactured fertilizers have a guaranteed analysis which is written on the package as a three number formulation, also known as the N-P-K ratio, which gives the percentage of each element. The first number of the formula is nitrogen, the most important ingredient for growth. The second number is phosphorus, which helps in fruit and flower production and promotes root growth. The third is potassium or potash, which is important for the root system where it modifies the absorption of water and the other elements necessary for growth.

A good fertilization program will be your single most important factor for producing lush and healthy plants and for reducing your time of production. All fertilizers will enhance the growth rate of plants, but their particular formulations promote growth at different rates.

Organic fertilizers are produced from the remains or by-products of once living organisms. They include blood meal (13-0-0), cottonseed meal (6-1-2), bone meal (0.5-15-0), fish emulsion (5-2-2) and all manures, whose analysis is not given on the bag, but is usually 1-1-1. You can see from the N-P-K numbers that organic fertilizers tend to be strong in only one element and generally lacking in the other two, or are low in all three elements. They release their nutrients slowly, are long lasting, and are less likely to burn tender plants. They should be used with vegetable starts which you want to keep strictly organic, but for general containerized nursery production organic fertilizers work too slowly and their formulations do not offer plants a balanced diet.

The nursery business grows on chemical fertilizers. These plant foods are applied in dry or liquid form. Granular fertilizers are applied dry either by sprinkling on the soil surface or by working into the soil. Water must be added after application. A liquid fertilizer comes in either a liquid form or a water soluble granule. It is mixed with water first and then applied to the soil or sprayed on the foliage. In either case it is water that transfers the nutrients to the plant. No fertilizer works without water.

For most plant production a balanced all-purpose fertilizer is sufficient, but there are also fertilizers specially formulated for specific types of plants; for example, acid loving plants like azaleas, camellias and rhododendrons have one formulation, citrus another. There are so many different formulas and specialty fertilizers that it is difficult to know which to choose. Since I went through a gamut of fertilizer types in a process of trial and error before I settled on one fertilizer that suited what I grew and how I operated, I will recount for you my experience.

I started using a granular fertilizer since it was fairly inexpensive and was easy to apply by simply sprinkling a small amount into the can on the soil surface. However, I found out that it is also very easy to over apply. One of the major mistakes made in using granular fertilizer is equating a plant in the ground with a plant in the container. When the directions on the bag give the application rates based on the height of the plant or the diameter of the trunk, they are talking about an established plant in the ground. The bag may tell you to sprinkle a half-pound of fertilizer around the base of a tree with a one-inch diameter trunk, but that will kill a one-inch tree in a five gallon container. You cannot use anywhere near the same amount of fertilizer on a plant in a container, whose roots are concentrated in a very small area, as on one in the ground.

The danger of over fertilizing becomes even greater when the nitrogen content is higher and when it is applied during hotter weather. You may not realize that you over-fertilized until several days later when the plants begin to brown out or turn black, a condition called fertilizer burn. At the least you have made the plants unmarketable and at the worst too much fertilizer will kill the plants. The only thing you can do to correct this mistake is to water the plants over and over again, trying to flush out that extra fertilizer. I usually learn my lessons the expensive way. I educated myself on a block of 500 plants.

Once burned by granular fertilizer, I looked for a safer way to fertilize. I next tried the liquids because they do not burn, if mixed properly. I mixed some up in gallon milk cartons and went from plant to plant. I had too many plants to spend that much time mixing. Although liquid fertilizer solved the problem of burning the plants, it was tedious watering each plant and it needed to be applied frequently. Nurseries which always use liquid fertilizer apply it through an injection system that puts the fertilizer directly into the water each time the plant is irrigated. In some nurseries you may have noted warnings on the faucets not to drink the water. The injection method works extremely well, but the systems the large growers use are very expensive to set up. There are less sophisticated systems available for home use which can be hooked up to a hose or sprinkler system. I, however, did not relish the thought of how much fertilizer I would be pouring on the ground during the overhead watering.

I decided to go back to granular fertilizer knowing that there were ways I could lessen my risk. I applied smaller amounts and used a fertilizer that contained less nitrogen. It worked. It did not burn the plants, but I found that it also meant that I had to fertilize more often. The problem with having to fertilize more often is that, if you do not get around to it, and of course I didn't, the plants just sit still waiting for their food. If they have to wait too long, and of course they did, they will actually begin to deteriorate. I now realized that no matter how good the fertilizer was, it would not work for me if I did not get around to using it. Since the plants needed to obtain a constant supply of nutrients in order to sustain any growth, and since I had to be careful not to apply too much fertilizer, I decided to try something that I had been avoiding because of the high cost, time release fertilizer.

This fertilizer is a granular pellet or prill which is coated by a resin shell that deteriorates slowly in order to allow only small amounts of the nutrients to become available at a time. There are a number of different brands with different formulas and varying periods of time release. There are also larger pellets in pre-measured doses which are added to the soil like a pill. Which you use depends on what you are growing and how long the plant may need to be held in a container until sold or replanted. Your type of soil may also affect the way the fertilizer works.

Time release fertilizer feeds the plants a steady diet. The advantage I found over other options is that you add the fertilizer to the soil at the time of planting and do not worry about it again. It does not burn and the plants grow at an even rate. For a year I resisted using time release fertilizer because of its seemingly high price. But when other fertilizers produced disappointing results, I spent the money and experimented. If you buy it in small boxes, your retail cost will run close to $4.00 per pound. Your best value is buying it in 50 lb. bags which cost about $1.00 per pound. At the dollar a pound rate it breaks down to between only $.04 and $.08 for the one to two tablespoons you use per gallon can.

Look for the trace elements sulfur and iron in the formulation. They are especially important in fertilizers used on container plants. Sulfur works together with nitrogen in the production of protoplasm and although common in the ground, it is very quickly leached out of the soil in containers by watering. It definitely helps to replace it through slow release. Iron helps maintain that bright green color that makes a plant look healthy and iron needs to be added to most composts.

So many nurseries now use time release fertilizer that it is fairly common to find the prills mixed into the container soil. Consistent success encouraged me to continue using time release fertilizer and my confidence in it was reaffirmed one particularly rainy spring. I had bought 800 bareroot birch trees in January, resold 100 to another nurseryman who had been buying them from me for the last three years; I canned the other 700 into #5s. When I was visiting my customer in May, he asked me, "What's wrong with the birch trees this year? They're not growing." I was quite surprised for I was very happy with mine which were only a few weeks from marketability. We walked out into his field to look at his trees. They looked healthy enough, but they were certainly smaller than mine. I assured him that my trees were growing just fine, so it could not be a problem with the original source of the trees. As we stood scratching our heads, the answer came to both of us at the same time. He applied his fertilizer through an injection system which put the fertilizer into the water. The plants were fertilized every time they were watered by that system, but because it had rained so much that spring, he had not needed to use the system as often. My trees had the time release fertilizer mixed into the soil and it fed them continuously whatever the water source.

This also points out another advantage of time release fertilizer. Plants grown on injection systems begin to use up their food quickly once removed from their fertilized water and consequently do not have long shelf lives. Time release fertilizer continues to feed the plant whether it is in your field or a retailer's sales yard or a customer's garden.

LABELS

One more key component going into the containerizing of the plant is the label or identification tag. This small piece of plastic or paper is of great importance because it identifies the plant for the customer. Nursery regulations require that each plant be labeled with the full name of the plant when it is offered for sale to the public. The labeling responsibility is placed on the grower since he is the one who is supposed to know what he has produced. Putting labels on at the time of canning is the best way to keep track when you have many varieties, but regulations require only that you tag the plants at the time of shipping.

Labels come in three basic forms: stakes which are inserted into the soil as with bedding plants, slip-on tags that go on a branch of the plant, and glue-on tags that go onto the containers. The simplest and least expensive tags are the unprinted stake or slip-on types which run only about a penny and a half each in 1,000 count bags or rolls. You simply write the plant name on the tag. Use an indelible pen or a pencil, not a ball point pen. Pre-printed labels cost only slightly more, but you may have to order in minimum quantities of 1,000 tags per variety. You may not produce that many plants of any one variety. As a marketing tool, a picture tag is one of the best investments you can make since it can help sell a plant not yet in bloom or one which has gone out of bloom. The costs start around $.06 each and range upwards depending on the size of the tag and planting information printed on it.

Some of your customers may require that the labels include the UPC bar code. These tags are also available from the label manufacturers. However, you must obtain your own bar code number from the Uniform Code Council, 8163 Old Yankee Road, Suite J, Dayton, Ohio 45458, Phone 513-435-3870. There is a one-time set up fee of $300.00.

THE DREADED W'S
Once you have found your sources for supplies, you need to plan how to deal with the three least appealing aspects of the nursery business, the three dreaded W's: watering, weeding, and waiting.

WATERING
The actual labor time it takes to put a plant into a container is measured in minutes and seconds, but the newly canned plant in most cases is not immediately marketable. Growing plants, unlike manufacturing a product, can take a long time. However, the truth is, you do none of the actual growing; the plant does all of that. You are doing the nurturing which requires a passage of time clocked in months. The plant's most basic need during this process of growing is an adequate supply of water. Once a plant has been containerized, its potential food and moisture sources are limited by the sides of its container. Unless the water gets directly into the rootball in the container, the plant has not been watered. The time a plant in a container can go without water cannot be equated with an established plant in the ground which has been able to expand its root system in search of its needs and can draw on other resources when the water does not fall from above. The soil in the nursery container has been chosen to drain well and a good portion of the water added to the soil does drain away immediately. Moreover, the black plastic containers can become very hot in the summer months and evaporate the water more quickly. If a plant is allowed to dry out and then to cook in the hot

container, it is only a short time before the plant has been damaged to the point of being unmarketable and only a slightly longer time until it is dead. The water needs of the plant will vary with the season and it is up to you to determine how often to water.

The easiest, least costly and most readily available way to irrigate your plants is with a hose. This water delivery system is a tried and true, non-technical, inexpensive method of watering plants. It is still one of the most widely practiced methods in most retail nurseries. In your visits to nurseries you may have seen someone watering with a water wand on the end of the hose. This is a long metal tube with a head on the end which works like a sieve to break up the force of the water so as not to wash away the soil. Sometimes a hand sprinkler is used to break the force of the water, but your own thumb is also effective in dispelling the water's force. Standing there at the end of a hose, watering your crop, can be a satisfying daily experience for the gardener who wants to see how the plants are growing and enjoy the changes. It is also a good way to keep track of potential problems.

However, not everyone is interested in this daily contact and there are alternative methods of watering to consider. The next least costly way to water is to have a sprinkler attached to the end of the hose and to let it water unattended. There are even battery-operated timer devices so that you do not have to go out to turn on the hose. This works well if you have plants grouped in a very small area, but if one sprinkler setting does not cover all the containers, the hose will have to be moved and in this case you might want to consider a more extensive sprinkler system with multiple heads which will cover the whole area in successive stages. An electronic timer can be used to completely automate the sprinklers. This type of system is quite effective on flats filled with bedding plants or liner stock or on young newly transplanted gallon containers, but sprinklers are not always efficient in getting the water into the cans of plants which are very full and bushy, or in getting the corners of rows, or in maintaining a steady stream of water on windy days; and invariably the plant that has fallen over is completely out of luck. Moreover, it is a very wasteful and inefficient way to water container material. Excessive runoff may irritate neighbors, and where water wasting is punished by fines, it can be expensive. If you are on a water meter, you will be paying for wasted water and the cost will be cutting into your profit.

This concern about water, and making sure that it gets to the plants and not the ground around them, has led to the third major type of water system used in wholesale nurseries, drip irrigation. Since each plant needs its own water emitter, this system is more costly in its initial set up. If you are growing hundreds of plants in #1 containers, it may not be the system you want to use, but it is particularly useful for plants in larger containers like #5s and #15s. However, although drip irrigation can be set on timers, it is not completely carefree. The emitters have to be kept in the containers and there are various reasons why they can and do come out of the containers or become clogged. Even if you use drip irrigation, you will need to check the system regularly to be sure that it is working properly. Nor can the drip irrigation pick up trees and shrubs that have blown over in the wind. Yet a good system once installed will eliminate the need for you to water daily by hand. The walk through to inspect the system and the plants can be a pleasurable stroll among your growing profits.

Another water saving method of irrigation useful to the small grower is root zone irrigation. A new system developed in Australia is generating a great deal of interest here. The "BottomUp" system consists of a lightweight, durable laminate of three materials, topped by a weed mat. Water is supplied by pipes down each side of the bed. Very little site preparation is necessary. You simply roll out the laminate bed, clip up the side pipes and put the plants on the mat. It can irrigate all types of pots up to 8" in diameter and saves at least 60% of the water used by traditional overhead sprinklers.

WEEDING

There is only one plant that seems to be able to completely fend for itself when it comes to water. Unfortunately, that plant is a weed. Whenever a plant dies, we move the container out of the row and set it aside until we get around to dumping it out. If there is a weed in the container, it seems to just go on living for weeks, despite receiving no water. There is no question that when it comes to weeds you are dealing with a formidable adversary. If allowed to grow in the container, they will steal both the water and the fertilizer that your money-making plant needs for growth. Weed control, then, is necessary, and although there are times when removing these troublemakers and returning order to the container garden can be very therapeutic in a transferred sort of way, it still remains a task few people look forward to or relish. However, there are ways to control weeds without constantly pulling them.

To begin with, you should do something to keep the weeds off the ground. This can be achieved in two ways, either with materials that cover the ground or with chemicals. Most gardeners are familiar with the graveled beds and walks in the retail nursery. A thick layer of gravel serves as an effective weed barrier and offers drainage of excess water; yet doing a large area in gravel is expensive and not as permanent as one might think. Gravel does sink into the wet soil and does have to be replenished.

An inexpensive and yet one of the most effective ground covering materials to prevent weeds is black plastic. We roll out six mil black plastic right over existing weeds and let the containers placed on the plastic smash the weeds down and level it out. However, since the plastic also prevents the water from being absorbed into the ground under the cans, water drains into the aisles making the areas where you walk muddier. Gravel in just the aisles solves this problem. Weed block fabrics which allow the water to permeate into the soil, but prevent the weeds from coming through, are alternatives to black plastic and are only slightly more expensive.

There are also chemical controls for weeds. The most familiar weed killers must be sprayed directly onto the weeds since they work by being absorbed through the foliage into the plant. There are selective killers that target only grass weeds and others that attack broad leaf weeds and others that kill everything they touch. When spraying the weeds on the ground it is very important to avoid getting any spray on the containerized stock. However, accidents do happen and if you are aware that you have sprayed a plant, usually you can correct the mistake by simply washing the spray off with water before it has time to dry on the plant. When the wind has caused drift which you do not notice and you allow the spray to dry on the affected plants, you may kill or severely damage your money crop. Most weed killers affect only what they touch, but there are other types of sprays which kill existing weeds and leave a chemical in the ground to attack the roots of any plant that tries to grow in the soil. These are useful where you want nothing to grow for about a year, but you do not want to use them where you are putting your containers. Like any prisoner, plants are anxious to escape from their holding cells and they frequently get their roots out into the ground through the drain holes. They will be seriously damaged or killed by chemicals that work on roots.

One of the ways to avoid frequent spraying of the growing weeds is to use chemicals which prevent seeds from germinating. These chemicals are called pre-emergents and are available in granular or liquid form. Pre-emergents will not attack growing plants, but when put on the ground, they set up a barrier on the surface of the ground which attacks the weed seed as it germinates, killing the plant before it can emerge as a problem. This principle can also be applied to the soil in the container itself. There are a variety of chemicals that prevent weed seeds from germinating in the can and do not hurt the plant. Such chemicals are not labeled for every type of plant so you have to read the label very carefully before applying.

Never use weed killer on a weed growing in the container. Weeds already growing in the can will have to be removed by hand. The chemicals that work in the containers are only pre-emergents and do not work on growing weeds. Some of the pre-emergents for nursery stock are fairly expensive, so you may prefer to just pull weeds by hand rather than go to this expense for prevention. Keeping the weeds off the ground so that they do not produce seeds to blow into the cans is one of the most effective preventive measures you can take. The second most important thing is to pull the weeds when they are young and small. It does not take a weed very long to grow to a good size, and if you let it get too big, it may entwine with the cutting or seedling and you may pull out your new plant with the weed. Once your plant has gotten big enough to cover the soil area of the container, it is much more difficult for weed seeds to find their way into the can.

WAITING

The third dreaded "W", waiting, can be the most intimidating of the three, even for a gardener who is prepared to wait. A gardener nurtures and tends plants with the expectation of receiving some return on labor either in the enjoyment of beautiful flowers or the shade of trees or the harvest of fruit and vegetables, but there is a limit to how long one will wait, how long one will nurture, how long one will tend before one reaps a reward. Some people buy tomato seeds, others buy young starts in six-packs; others want larger four-inch pots, and there are even those who want gallon size or larger plants with tomatoes already on them. The essential nature of the plant never changes; a tomato plant is always a tomato plant, the only thing that has been added in each successive stage is time and that is what accounts for the increase in price at each stage. The same holds true for all types of plant material. Understanding this relationship of time to money is the key to understanding the nature of the nursery business. The product that the nursery customer buys is a plant, but what the nurseryman is really selling is time.

By paying attention to the proper details, anyone can start and grow plants, but very few people want to take the time to start at the beginning. It is just a lot easier to go down to the nursery and buy a plant that already has some size to it rather than throw a seed into the ground and wait for it to grow. Most customers consider it a bargain that someone else has spent the months or years necessary to get the product to size. Indeed, if it is such a bargain for the customer, where does the grower come out on this transaction? A long time can pass with watering and weeding and who wants to wait a long time for a payday? But just as there are ways around the tedium of watering and weeding, there are ways to shorten the growing time and hasten the payday.

There are three major ways to speed up your production time: 1) have a good fertilization program, 2) use microclimates to produce a longer growing period and 3) start with plants already further along in the growing process. We have discussed fertilizer and micro-climates in Chapter One, yet the third way to speed along growing time may be the most profitable for the backyard nurseryman. Buying plants from other growers allows you to bypass those stages of production which you are not equipped to handle. Let other growers use the greenhouse, let other growers work large tracts of land, let other growers spend two years producing seedlings. In turning a pastime into a business there may be large gaps in your knowledge or experience, but you do not have to know how to do everything in order to go into the nursery business. The subsequent chapters will show how the growing of plants can be broken down into stages which allow you to continue doing what is familiar, to learn through experience what is not already known and to invest in other people's time and expertise to help your nursery grow.

CHAPTER 3

STAGE ONE: THE BEGINNING

CREATION OF THE NEW PLANT
In the next five chapters, the process of growing plants in containers is broken down into a series of five stages corresponding to container sizes in ascending order. As the size of the container increases, so must the size of the plant which is to fill out that container. Growing a larger plant increases the waiting time. The next five chapters break down the growing process into a series of progressive stages showing the backyard nurseryman how to enter into the production process at any point and produce marketable plants in each stage within a single growing season, thus reducing the time spent waiting for your profit.

This chapter treats Stage One where the plant begins. It is the least expensive stage in which to start your business and it can also be one of the most satisfying experiences for the grower. Plants in this stage are sold in the smallest sizes of nursery containers, such as cell-packs, liner pots and four-inch pots. The material produced in Stage One can either be sold or moved into another stage of production. The plant must start in Stage One, but it is possible for you to start in any of the other four stages by using material grown by another producer in an earlier stage.

Although there are thousands of different plants growing in the world, they can be divided into just three basic categories:

annuals, biennials and perennials. Annuals are plants whose life cycle is limited to one year or less, such as marigolds, petunias, pansies, snapdragons and vegetables. Biennials are plants, such as foxglove and Canterbury bells, whose life cycle is just two years. These plants do not bloom until their second year and then die. Perennials, in the broadest sense, are plants whose life cycle is more than two years.

ANNUALS

We begin our discussion with annuals. According to the plans devised by nature, annuals on their death leave behind them the seeds from which the new generation of plants will sprout in the following spring. The seeds lie dormant through the winter months waiting for the weather to warm and the days to grow longer before the new plants put down roots and then sprout their new leaves. The whole cycle begins anew. Nature's cycle of planned obsolescence has proven very profitable for the nursery industry. Every year the gardener replaces the dead annuals, either from seed or from starter plants purchased from a nursery, making the sale of annuals a mainstay of the industry. Some of the most common annuals are listed in Tables 3.1 and 3.2.

Table 3.1 Common flowering annuals

ageratum	impatiens	salvia
alyssum	lobelia	snapdragon
aster	marigold	stock
begonia semperflorens	pansy	verbena
calendula	petunia	vinca rosea
celosia	phlox	viola
coleus	poppy	zinnia
dahlia	portulaca	
dianthus	primrose	

Table 3.2 Common vegetable starts

broccoli	cucumber	squash
cabbage	eggplant	tomato
cantaloupe	lettuce	watermelon
cauliflower	onion	
corn	pepper	

PRODUCTION OF ANNUALS FROM SEED

Most gardeners are familiar with the wide variety of seeds offered for sale in the retail stores and mail order catalogues. A great deal of information is available on those packets of seeds. Spend some time at a seed rack looking at the pictures of the plants and read the backs of the packages of those which interest you. Generally, they tell you when to plant the seeds and how long it takes for them to germinate. Some give a color coded reference map of the United States with suggested outdoor planting times. In some parts of the country the growing season for annuals starts in mid-March, in other areas May. Yet, the simplest planting advice given on the packages is to wait until all danger of frost is past. For sowing seeds in the garden this is good advice, but it takes into consideration only the safety of the plant, not someone's desire to make money on the plant.

When the seed packages indicate that it is safe for the seed to sprout, the greenhouse growers already have their first plants on the market. They started their petunias ten to twelve weeks before, the marigolds eight to twelve weeks before and the tomatoes five to seven weeks before. If you plant your seeds the day the greenhouse growers are offering their first plants for sale, you have to wait these same number of weeks for your plants to reach marketable size. A considerable portion of the prime marketing time may pass before your product is ready. If you want to grow annuals and market them in any large quantity, you will need to use some kind of artificial climate. The primary benefit of a greenhouse is that its modified climate provides the heat necessary to germinate seeds. However, in many areas a cold frame can accomplish the same thing. The greenhouse climate also eliminates all fear of frost and its warm temperatures promote steady growth of the seedlings. In many areas a plastic house, even when it cannot provide the temperatures necessary for germination, can provide frost protection for seedlings which have been germinated in a greenhouse or cold frame. Use of cold frames, plastic houses and insulation fabrics adds several weeks of growing time to the beginning of the annual season.

If you do not want to use some kind of artificial climate to overcome cold and frost danger, your production of annuals from seeds has to follow nature's own cycle waiting for warmer weather. This has obviously worked well for nature for eons, but then she never had business considerations.

In the warmer climates, there is a second bedding plant season in the fall for the cool weather flowers and vegetables, such as pansies, violas, broccoli, and cabbage. Since seeds for these late season crops are sown in the summer, cold weather is not a factor in their germination. Instead, growers must be careful of the summer heat. Not only is drying and burning a real danger, but the plants can also grow too quickly, becoming leggy, or bloom too early and go to seed. Shade cloth becomes essential in order to protect the plants from heat and to control growth.

Most retail packages of seeds contain only a few grams or milligrams. Even these small amounts can produce a good number of plants since many varieties of flower seeds are very tiny; for example, alyssum is estimated at 90,000 seeds/oz., snapdragons at 180,000/oz. and petunias at 285,000/oz. When you first begin to grow annuals, you may want to buy your seeds in small retail quantities. You can cut your cost by watching for sales at the beginning of the season. We have frequently seen some brand name seeds discounted as much as 50% in the drug and grocery stores. Sometimes you can find some very inexpensive seeds priced at $.10 to $.20 per package. These may be lesser known economy brands marked down for promotional sales, but just because they are cheaper brands does not mean that they will not grow nice plants. Their germination rate, however, may be somewhat less than better known brands and the selection is very limited. Popularity determines how well certain varieties sell, so if you grow varieties that the nurseries do not even want to carry, you may find your bargain seeds very difficult to sell as plants. In making your choices, consider where you will be selling the plants.

It may be particularly profitable to identify specialty niches. For example, there may be a strong demand for ethnic vegetables not commonly found, or while many growers are rushing to produce the newest varieties of vegetables on the market, there is an ever increasing demand for the reintroduction of older heirloom varieties. Such seeds are available by mail from several sources such as Seeds of Change in Santa Fe, New Mexico, but the ready grown plants are seldom offered in retail nurseries.

Let your first year of growing annuals be a learning experience and do not go overboard in buying large quantities of seeds and supplies. If you find you are successful and intend to produce a large quantity of flats of annual color or vegetables in the next season, you do not want to continue paying retail prices for your seeds. Request a wholesale catalogue. You can find any company's address on the retail seed packets. Some companies charge a fee for their wholesale catalogues which may be a wealth of information, not only giving you pictures of the flowers, but also telling you how many seeds there are to an ounce, germination time, the amount necessary to propagate given numbers of flats and the growing time to salable plants.

You may be wondering if you really have to buy seeds or if you can save them from annuals. You have to be aware of one important fact about modern flowers and vegetables. More and more nursery stock is germinated from hybrid seeds. A hybrid is a distinct plant which was produced by cross-pollinating two species, varieties, subspecies, strains or any combination of these. The new plant is different from both of its parents. Its seeds in turn will produce plants different from itself and may even revert back to the grandparents or be something different again. You cannot be sure what you will get with the seeds from hybrid plants. If you want the next generation of flowers to look like the picture on the package from which the first generation came or for the vegetable to taste the same as what you grew, you better get another package of the same hybrid seeds and forget the ones on the plants.

In cases where you know for a fact that the plants are not hybrids and that they have not been pollinized by another variety, you can harvest the seeds and your plants will come true to their own characteristics. In harvesting and using your own seed, proper handling and storage are important for viability. Any number of factors destroy the ability of the seeds to germinate. Store in a cool, dry place and leave the container open to the air. If the container must be sealed in order to provide protection from insects or rodents, be sure the seeds are dry when sealed. And then, of course, come spring, not remembering where you put the seeds last winter is the final straw that drives most of us to rely on professional seed dealers.

PLANTING YOUR SEEDS
Once you have determined what to grow, how do you plant the seeds? When you see annuals offered for sale at the nurseries, they are usually in six-packs or four-inch pots. The large growers use planting machines costing thousands of dollars to fill the flats with soil and plant the seeds, but before the invention of these machines people used their hands and followed nature's lead with planting instructions. Nature has several methods of planting. Marigold seeds ripen and dry, and as the flower dries, the pod bends over and dumps the seeds on the ground. Impatiens seed pods, on the other hand, dry and constrict until torsion forces the pod to burst open and hurl the seeds away from the plant. The one thing that a plant does not

do is make a hole in the ground and put in the seed. If you try to plant the tiny seeds one to each cell in a flat, not only will you spend a great deal of time separating seed, but you will be wasting time since a percentage of them will wash out or simply not germinate. Planting seeds one at a time only works well with larger seeds, such as melon and squash, which are generally planted two or three seeds to a two-inch or four-inch pot.

The easiest way to plant seeds is to follow nature's lead. First, fill a 17" square flat with soil. It is important that the soil for seeds be a loose, light mix. If you use time release fertilizer, mix it into your soil according to directions before planting. Leave a little room at the top of the flat and compact the soil. Simply scatter the seeds evenly over the soil. You may use several packets of seed per flat. Add a 1/8" layer of soil over the sown seed to give additional protection and warmth.

In order for seeds to germinate they need warm temperatures; for example, alyssum and pansies need only 60°, but impatiens, marigolds, petunias and tomatoes need ten more degrees. You can provide inexpensive heat artificially by using a cold frame for germination. In a very small cold frame, you can germinate thousands of seeds in just a few flats.

You have to wait until the seedlings put on their second or even third tier of leaves before they are big enough to transplant into the containers in which they will be sold. For those who do not want to go to the trouble of creating artificial climates, there is another option besides waiting for nature to generate the seeds in her own time.

STARTER PLUGS

You can purchase annuals already germinated and growing. Many of the seed companies have expanded their market by selling plugs. Seeds are planted by machine into seedling trays with very tiny cells. One type of flat has 288 cells which are only 3/4" wide x 1 3/4" deep and another flat has 512 smaller cells only 1/2" wide x 3/4" deep. The cost of plugs in the 512 cell flats is in the range of $.03 to $.09; the plugs in the 288 cell flats cost between $.11 and $.19. Plug growers know that not every cell is filled with a plant, so many tend to round out the counts and lower the price of the flat. Any order for plugs must be placed in advance. Plug flats are not sitting on tables waiting for a buyer, but are custom grown to your order. A grower plants your seeds and several weeks later the flats are shipped out to you. They are frequently shipped air freight since tiny plugs cannot go long without moisture. Ground shipments can travel to your door via Federal Express and UPS. Once you receive the plugs, transplant them as quickly as possible into jumbo six-packs or four-inch pots since the tiny rootballs do dry out rapidly.

Buying any type of starter plants is a trade-off for the nurseryman. It costs a certain amount of money to produce a plant: the seed, the soil, the fertilizer, greenhouse overhead, as well as some loss factor. When these costs and risks have been undertaken by someone else, you pay a higher price plus shipping, but you do only pay for success.

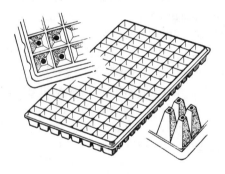

Starter plug flat cells

CONTAINERS FOR ANNUALS

There are several types of packaging for annuals. They are usually offered in plastic six-packs or as individual plants in two-inch or four-inch cells or pots. The six-packs and pots are held in plastic flats. Cell packaging of annuals uses two components: the holding flat plus the insert, which is a single sheet of plastic molded into cell packs or individual cells. The plants are sold by the flat or the cell packs can be separated and sold individually. Pricing for some units are listed in Table 3.3.

Table 3.3 Containers for annuals

Type of Container	Flat Size	# per case	Unit Price
Bedding Flat	11" x 21"	100	$0.53
Insert	**Cell Size**		
6 six cell	5 1/4" x 7"	100	$0.41
8 six-pack insert	5 1/4" x 5 1/4"	100	$0.35
36 sgl. cell insert	2 5/8" x 2 1/4"	100	$0.35
17" square flat	17 "x 17"	80	$0.45
Insert	**Cell Size**		
6 pony six-pack	5" x 7 3/4"	100	$0.44
16 4" cell packs	4" x 4"	120	$0.44
25 3" cell packs	3" x 3"	60	$0.49

The combined cost of the two piece unit of any of these six types of flats is under $1.00, that is, the price of the holding flat plus the insert. The 17" square flats are also used for holding twenty-five individual 3" pots or sixteen 4" pots, which can be purchased for $.06 and $.09 respectively. It is possible for you to get better prices for quantity, but it is also possible for you to get some of this plastic for free. Since the inserts are designed to be sold separately, they are frequently removed from the holding flat and the empty flats pile up at retail nurseries. Used four-inch pots are also frequently available. Sometimes the wholesale grower returns to collect the empties, but just as frequently they are thrown into the garbage. Almost every retail nursery creates a good supply of plastic containers that it does not need or use or want. Talk to the owner or the manager of the nursery department to see what arrangement you can make.

32 Liner Tray   *32 Pots - Cut*

Inserts for bedding flats

TRANSPLANTING THE SEEDLINGS

When you are ready to transplant the seedlings or plugs into flats, begin by putting the insert into the holding flat, fill the insert with your bedding soil mixed with fertilizer and press it down. Water it. Next make a hole in the wet soil in the center of each cell with a stick about the width of your little finger. From your seedling flat break off a portion of the soil with the plants. Carefully separate the seedlings and stick one into each hole in the cell packs. If the roots have gotten slightly larger than the hole, expand its width by routing it out with a few extra turns of the stick. Plugs are planted the same way. One trick to get the hole the right size is to cut off one of the tiny cells and jam it onto the end of the stick you are using to poke the holes. Now you have a punch just the right size. After inserting the seedling, it is important to get the dirt to fill in around the roots. Use your fingers to press down the dirt around the seedlings and water the flat. The flow of the water will also move the dirt in around the roots.

If some seedlings have developed root systems too large to fit easily into the small holes made by your stick, plant them into 3" or 4" pots. Instead of stuffing the roots into a premade hole in the soil, use an empty container. Hold the plant between your thumb and index finger to keep it upright and steady in the center of the empty container and pour in dry soil around the roots, press the soil in around the plant and water. Watering shortly after planting is most important to successful transplanting.

PRODUCTION OF PERENNIALS

The term perennials in nursery vernacular has come to refer to a large group of herbaceous flowering plants most of which die down to the ground during the winter and return the following spring. But in the broadest sense, as used here under this general heading, perennials include all plants which live more than two years. The seasonal time factor is not as important in the production of perennials as it is with annuals. Since perennials do not die at the end of a year's cycle, their marketing time is not limited to only one season. If they do not sell in their prime market season, the plants continue to grow larger and can be sold in another season, or transferred to a larger container, or even used to propagate new plants, whereas any unsold annuals become garbage. Market timing is less critical with perennials.

HERBACEOUS PERENNIALS FROM SEED

We begin our discussion with that group of herbaceous, or non-woody, flowering plants which are now commonly called "perennials" in the industry and in gardening books. A list of some common varieties propagated from seed, cuttings and division is given in Table 3.4. The popularity of these plants has steadily grown over the years as more and more gardeners see in perennials an alternative to annuals which must be replaced yearly or seasonally. Like annuals, many perennials are propagated from seeds. Return again to the retail seed racks and look at the large selection of perennial seeds. Most companies clearly mark their packets PERENNIAL right on the top. On the back they give planting directions and germination times.

Sowing the seeds and transplanting the seedlings is similar to planting annuals. The main difference is that perennials germinate at lower temperatures and take slightly longer to sprout than annuals. Perennials are usually transplanted into jumbo packs or four-inch pots and bring a higher price than annuals. Unlike annuals, many perennials do not bloom in their first year. This does not help with marketing in these smaller sizes since many perennials are rather unattractive without flowers. The picture tag becomes an essential tool in marketing perennials out of bloom and is worth the extra five or six cents.

Table 3.4   Common herbaceous perennials

achillea	dianthus	moraea
agapanthus	dicentra	oenothera
androsace	fuchsia	paeonia
anemone	gaillardia	papaver
aquilegia	gaura	phlox
armeria	geranium	physostegia
artemisia	geum	platycodon
asparagus ferns	gypsophila	primula
astilbe	heliotropium	rudbeckia
bergenia	helleborus	scabiosa
campanula	hemerocallis	sedum
centaurea	hibiscus	solidago
chrysanthemum	hosta	stokesia
clivia	iberis	strelitzia
convolvulus	iris	tradescantia
coreopsis	lavandula	trollius
coronilla	liriope	verbena
delphinium	lupinus	vinca

Perennials are also available in plugs, ranging in sizes from the tiny 512 cells per flat to larger 36 cells per flat. Table 3.5 gives a price range for plugs in varying size cells.

A good way to find the widest selection of material is to contact a plant broker who represents a number of different growers. Some distributors of nursery supplies also broker starter plants.

Table 3.5 Perennial plug pricing

cells per flat	512	288	200	92	70	52	36
price range	.06-.12	.11-.19	.14-31	0.29	.31-.43	.31-.43	.69-.79

WOODY ORNAMENTALS FROM SEED

A large number of woody ornamentals and conifers are also propagated from seeds; however, these seeds are not found on retail racks. Most of these seeds are collected from the natural landscape rather than commercially grown. Many opportunities exist for you to collect your own seeds since far fewer species of woody ornamentals are hybridized. Although propagation by seed does not produce genetically identical offspring, your new plant will exhibit characteristics similar to the parent, so the source is important. If you collect seeds from weak, scraggly plants, the plants you propagate may exhibit the same unattractive characteristics as they grow older. Look for the best specimen that you can find. The seeds are there for the taking and it is not likely that you will have to fight off hoards of other people waiting for the liquidambar or the maple seeds to ripen. If you wish to harvest and use these gifts of nature, you must know the season when they ripen and collect the seeds before they have been scattered on the ground or blown away by the winds or eaten by the birds.

Seeds for woody ornamentals are also available commercially, collected from the wild by professional seed gatherers. Supplies are usually small and sell out quickly, so orders must be placed early. Seeds of woody ornamentals are quite a bit larger than annual and herbaceous perennial seeds and are sold by the pound, for example, red maple seeds cost about $15.00/lb., silver maple $4.00/lb., European white birch, $10.00/lb. and mugo pine $95.00/lb. Some of the more common woody ornamentals grown in liner pots from seed are listed in Table 3.6.

Table 3.6
Common woody ornamentals grown in liners from seed

acacia	eucalyptus	pistacia chinensis
acer	fraxinus	rhamnus
albizia	ginkgo	rhus
alnus	gordonia	robinia
bauhinia	grevillea	sapium
betula	jacaranda	schinus
cassia	koelreuteria	sophora
celtis	lagerstroemia	sorbus
ceratonia	laurus	tabebuia
cercis	liquidambar	ulmus
cinnamomum	magnolia	zelkova
cornus	nandina	
eriobotrya	nyssa sylvatica	

PLANTING THE SEEDS

Seeds may be planted in 17" square flats first, like the annuals, and then transplanted into containers. The containers used for woody ornamentals in Stage One are two-inch liner pots or peat pots. Very seldom are four-inch pots used. The liner pots are also held in 17" square flats which accommodate between 49 and 64 pots. Various types of liner pots are listed in Table 3.7.

The seeds of many woody ornamentals are large enough to separate by hand, so it is much easier to plant the liner pots individually with one seed each, saving the extra step of transplanting. However, experience is a bitter pill as well as a valuable teacher. On one occasion we collected deodar cedar seeds and planted each one individually into 500 liner pots. Only two seeds sprouted. Had we sown the seeds into two flats the time factor for our unfruitful labor would have been considerably less. Therefore, you should have great confidence in the viability of your seed before you spend time separating and planting each seed into liners.

Table 3.7   Liner pots

wide	deep	quantity/case	price/1,000
2"	2 1/8"	1548	$26.00
2 1/4"	2 1/2"	950	$34.00
2 3/4"	2 7/8"	984	$52.00
2 1/4" rose	3 1/4"	950	$47.00
2 3/8" tree	5"	325	$91.00
2 7/8" tree	9"	150	$190.00

GERMINATING SEED OF WOODY ORNAMENTALS

Many techniques of controlled seed germination for woody ornamentals are designed to speed up or override the natural process. Mechanical and acid scarification are processes which crack or soften the hard, impermeable seed coverings, thus making it easier for the embryo to emerge. Cold stratification, which is the layering of seeds in sand that is refrigerated at temperatures between 32 and 50 degrees or held outdoors over winter, is used to overcome dormancy of the embryo. Such processes usually produce prompt and uniform germination of seeds when planted. However, in the absence of specific knowledge as to which method is best for any particular species, it is simplest to follow the natural process as closely as possible. This means planting spring ripening seeds shortly after harvest and letting them germinate immediately; for fall ripening seeds, plant shortly after harvest and leave virtually unprotected in the flat through the winter until the longer days and warmer weather of spring trigger natural germination. Once the seeds have germinated, then additional frost protection may be necessary.

PROPAGATION BY CUTTINGS

Greater numbers of hard and soft wood ornamentals are propagated by cuttings than by seeds, including many herbaceous flowering perennials. Making plants by cuttings is a type of cloning whereby a piece of plant tissue is used to reproduce a whole plant. If a stem cutting is used, new roots must be generated; with a root cutting, new stems and leaves must be generated. With some plants even leaf cuttings are used. If you have never tried starting a new plant by cuttings, begin by experimenting with some plants that root easily. My first propagating experience at a nursery was planting flats of edulis iceplant. I was shown how to make a cutting and given a demonstration of how to poke my finger into the soil to make the hole and then insert the cutting. Management then left me to my job to repeat the process ninety-nine more times until one flat was filled, and then fifty more flats. It was a gratifying experience for me to see all 5,000 of those cuttings live and eventually see the flats sold. It really builds confidence to find that you actually do have a green thumb. What they had not told me was that I could have dropped edulis iceplant on concrete and it would have still put out roots.

Experimentation costs you nothing but your time. The physical process of making the cutting and inserting it into a rooting medium is simply a process of repetition. You will find that there are plants that you can easily propagate and others that books say are easy, but you just cannot get. The major thing that experience teaches you is what type of tissue to look for and what time of year to take the cuttings.

There are a large number of books on propagation on the market which you can consult for specific information on the plants you want to grow. One of the best textbooks on nursery propagation is *Plant Propagation, Principles and Practice* by Hudson T. Hartmann, Dale E. Kester and Fred T. Davies, Jr.

When it comes to finding cutting material, the world is your oyster. However, there is one area in which you want to be careful. Whereas propagation by seed is considered sexual reproduction, propagation using the plant's own tissue is called asexual reproduction. The prefix "a" is from Greek and simply means "without". Propagation "without sex" means tissue cloning. Perhaps you have seen a tag on a plant that read, "Asexual reproduction of this plant is prohibited by law." That is a patent tag. That tag serves notice to other growers that the developer of that plant variety has the exclusive right to its reproduction, which he can either do himself or sell the rights to other growers who pay royalties on the plants produced. A patent tag must accompany a plant reproduced and sold under that variety name. Most people are familiar with patented roses and are aware that they cost more than non-patented varieties, but any new variety of plant can be patented by its developer. Patented plants are not the gift of nature but the work of man and since we are in search of free gifts and not lawsuits for patent infringement, we are not interested in collecting this type of cutting material. Besides, nature provides countless other varieties with no strings attached, except the little rule we noted about seeds. The new plant created from the mother will be of identical genetic material and will exhibit identical traits, so here too you want to look for that outstanding specimen. A ready source of material may be found in your own yard, or a friend's or neighbor's. Treasures may be found in the gutters awaiting clean-up by city refuse crews. Landscape maintenance workers clip and trim bushes around shopping centers and office complexes and would not mind one bit if you hauled off a part of the clippings.

Cuttings should be as fresh as possible. If you have come upon an unexpected bonanza and cannot get back to plant the material within a short time, wrap it in paper and wet it down to keep the leaves from drying out. Once prepared, cuttings are usually put into flats filled with one or more of three different rooting media: sand, perlite, or vermiculite. Experimentation tells you which works best for the plants you propagate. Sand is the only one of the three readily found in bulk, but usually only small quantities of these media are needed so they are best purchased by the bag.

Line the bottom of a flat with a single sheet of newspaper before you fill it with your rooting medium. Then thoroughly soak the medium with water so that the holes you poke for the cuttings retain their shape. A 17" square flat holds 100 cuttings in 10 rows of 10. This leaves plenty of room for each cutting, but you can double this number with good results depending on what you are rooting. Each cutting should be dipped into a rooting hormone before planting to insure a good success rate. A small jar which will do thousands of cuttings can be purchased for around $5.00 per bottle retail.

The most important thing in maintaining your cuttings is to make sure they do not dry out. Moisture retention depends on the season and the type of protection you provide. The greatest success at rooting cuttings is found in greenhouses because they can maintain the humidity that keeps the tissue moist and provide the warmth that promotes rapid root growth. The backyard grower can use this principle on a much smaller, less expensive scale by using a cold frame. The enclosed microclimate of a cold frame keeps moisture from evaporating and the flats of cuttings may not need to be watered daily. When trying to generate roots in colder weather, you can also use a propagating mat or a heating cable under the flats. These work like electric blankets for plants, only they go under the bed, not on top. By providing heat to the bottom of the flat, they encourage more rapid rooting in cooler weather.

If you are propagating cuttings in the warmer months, the best way to protect your cuttings is to make a shade house by completely enclosing a frame with shade cloth. In an area of 6' by 6' you can get sixteen flats which easily hold over 2,000 cuttings. The shade cloth also offers some protection against frosts, making it functional as a year-round covering in some climates. The flats need more watering in a shade house than in a cold frame and should be checked daily. In hotter weather they should be sprinkled several times daily.

With some plants, propagation is possible without any kind of protective covering if you simply maintain enough moisture in the medium. I quite by accident found I had much better success rooting oleander cuttings with the flats on concrete in the full sun instead of under shade cloth. Verbena, too, rooted more quickly in the sun on the concrete. Experimentation will always uncover new and successful methods of propagation which will never be found in books.

Once rooted, the cuttings are transplanted into liner pots. Usually the root systems will be too large to fit into a pre-made hole so position the rooted cutting in the empty liner pot and hold it there while pouring in the dry soil around the roots. Press the soil down. Water each flat as you finish.

Most liner stock is grown to be transferred into larger containers by the original grower or it is sold to another grower who transplants it. With the exception of house plants, see Table 3.8, and bonsai starters, very few liner plants are sold on the retail market.

Flat grown seedlings separated for planting into liners.

Table 3.8 House plants sold in liners

abutilon	crossandra	maranta leuconeura
acalypha hispida	croton	neoregelia
achimenes	davallia	nephrolepis
adiantum	dieffenbachia	oxalis
aeschynanthus	dipladenia	peperomia
aglaonema modestum	dizygotheca	philodendron
aphelandra	dracaena	pilea cadierei
araucaria excelsa	echeveria	plectranthus australis
ardisia	epidendrum radicans	pothos
asplenium nidus	episcia	rhoeo spathacea
begonia	euphorbia pulcherrima	saintpaulia ionantha
bromeliad	ficus benjamina	sansevieria
browallia	ficus elastica	saxifraga sarmentosa
cactus	ficus lyrata	schefflera
caladium	fittonia	schlumbergera
calathea makoyana	gynura aurantiaca	sinningia
capsicum	haworthia	spathiphyllum
chlorophytum	helxine soleirolia	streptocarpus
cissus antarctica	hoya	syngonium
cissus rhombifolia	howea	tradescantia
coleus	kalanchoe	
crassula argentea	koeleria	

GROUND COVER FLATS

There is one category of perennials which is propagated mostly by cuttings and sold at this early stage of growth. This group of plant material is called ground cover. The most common ground cover used today is grass, but what is referred to as ground cover in the nursery industry is any kind of plant whose spreading habit makes it an attractive alternative to grass. A list of common ground covers is given in Table 3.9.

When fairly large areas of ground are to be covered, a very large number of plants is needed. The only way to keep land-scaping costs down is to purchase these plants in smaller sizes at smaller prices. This desire on the part of the consumer to save money has created a good demand for ground cover flats.

Occasionally ground covers are sold in liners, but most usually the plants come in 17" square flats. There are also quarter-flat plastic inserts available for the flats, which cost an additional $.55 but allow the flat to be divided without damage to the rest of the plants. It is also possible to use the plastic six-packs popular with the annuals.

Table 3. 9 Common ground cover plants grown in flats

ajuga	hedera	potentilla
arenaria	herniaria	rosmarinus
armeria	hypericum	sagina
baccharis	iceplant	sedum
campanula	isotoma	thyme
cerastium	lonicera	verbena
erodium	muehlenbeckia	veronica
festuca	ophiopogon	vinca
fragaria	osteospermum	viola
gazania	polygonum	zoysia

Since most of the varieties of ground cover are propagated in the container in which they are sold, a very loose soil mix, yet one which retains moisture, is needed for the cuttings. This may require special mixing of your planting soil with additional soil amendments. To promote quick rooting, growers frequently use plastic houses and then transfer the flats outside in order to acclimate them to outdoor weather conditions. In warmer weather, shade cloth helps keep the flats from drying out.

The number of plants in a ground cover flat varies depending on the species grown; some are 49 count, others are 64 or 81 or 100 count. The square roots of these numbers are 7, 8, 9 and 10, forming rows 7 x 7, 8 x 8, 9 x 9, and 10 x 10.

Planting ground cover flats is a labor-intensive operation requiring the mixing of the soil, the collection of cutting material, the preparation of the cuttings and finally the planting of usually 49 to 100 cuttings per flat. Working at a consistent pace you can do three to four 81 or 100 count flats in an hour. The normal wholesale price for a flat is $7.00 to $8.00, but the plants more difficult to root sell for more. On the per unit basis you get only between $.07 to $.16 per cutting, but if you consider your labor on an hourly basis, you can produce $21.00 to $28.00 worth of plant material per hour. Growing time is short and watering can be done easily by overhead sprinklers. Ground cover flats do provide a reasonable return for your time unless you have to replant many flats which have excessive loss.

The main challenge in ground cover production is finding an adequate supply of propagating material. Remember, the flats need 49 to 100 cuttings each. Maintenance landscapers who take care of very large commercial projects where they have to constantly trim ground covers can help you here. They may be quite willing to let you gather up and carry away the cuttings.

PROPAGATION BY DIVISION
The third most common method of nursery propagation is division which is quite literally a stock split, the dividing of one plant into two or more. Division produces fully viable plants which already have roots. A large number of flowering, herbaceous perennials can be propagated by division such as astilbe, daylilies and columbine. Many plants can be dug from the landscape and divided into smaller plants for canning into containers and the rest replanted in the ground. When plants already growing in containers are divided, the new production is

generally just a lateral move, not a step up to a larger container. In other words, if you divide a four-inch pot, you end up with new plants suitable for replanting into four-inch pots and the plants divided out from gallon containers are replanted into gallons. A forked weeding prong is a good tool to use for separating container plants. Division is one of the faster methods to produce a plant because you have a fully developed small plant right at the start and are not waiting for the development of a new root system or foliage. On the other hand, fewer plants can be propagated from the mother plant by division than from seeds or cuttings.

Daylilies divided from one gallon plant

OTHER METHODS OF PROPAGATION

The three methods of propagation discussed in this chapter do not cover all the ways plants are commercially produced, but seeds, cuttings and division are the most basic methods of propagation used in large scale nursery production. Layering, which is a method of propagation similar in principle to making cuttings, is used to develop roots on a stem while it is still on the parent plant. Instead of cutting it completely off the plant, the stem is bent or broken and the wound is covered by soil or another moisture retaining medium. The mother plant continues to feed the stem while it begins to develop roots at the wound. Once it has new roots the stem can be cut below the roots and transplanted. Layering involves more labor, requires more space than cuttings, and is unnecessary with the vast majority of plants, but is useful on clones which will not root easily from cuttings.

Grafting and budding are not covered in this book. The principles and methods of grafting can be found in Hartmann, Kester and Davies' book and other books specialize in the topic. As you become more familiar with plants and the marketplace, grafting is one area of specialization you may want to consider.

In any method of propagation experienced gardeners have some tricks of their own. To use these tricks to generate salable nursery stock is to profit from your experience. To attempt things yet untried will only give you more experience, telling you what will and what won't work for you. While one person may find propagating successful and rewarding, another may be frustrated and defeated. In one area the climate may be amenable to backyard propagation, in another hostile. But as we said at the beginning, although the plant may have to start in Stage One, a nurseryman does not, and we are now ready to look into Stage Two.

CHAPTER 4

STAGE TWO: GALLON CONTAINERS

The containers discussed in Stage Two are essentially variations of one gallon pots, also called #1s. A sampling is given in Table 4.1.

Table 4.1 #1 containers

type of pot	wide	deep	capacity	# per case	unit price
black plastic	6"	5"	119 cu. in.	100	$.17
black plastic	6"	7"	183 cu. in.	100	$.20
blow molded black plastic	6 7/8"	6 1/2"	137 cu. in.	100	$.16
pulp	6"	6"	159 cu. in.	135	$.23
green/white	5 1/2"	4 3/8"	76 cu. in.	306	$.11
green/white	6"	4 1/2"	91 cu. in.	300	$.13
green/white	6 1/2"	5"	122 cu. in.	330	$.13
green/white	6"	6"	152 cu. in.	200	$.22
used #1s					$.05

The black plastic and molded pulp containers are widely used for landscape flowers, shrubs and trees; the round green and round white pots make a more decorative presentation and are generally used for house plants, azaleas, mums and other floral plants. Annuals are transplanted into any of these three types.

A standard gallon sized container is the 6" x 7" black plastic pot with a 183 cu. in. capacity. Once planted, it weighs about five to six pounds, depending on the proportions of mineral and organic materials in the mix. A cubic foot of soil has 1728 cu. in. Allowing for some unfilled space at the top of a gallon can, in order to leave room for water, you can fill about ten gallon cans with one cubic foot of soil. There are 27 cu. ft. in a cubic yard, so you get about 270 gallons from one yard of soil. Calculate your per unit cost by dividing the cost of a yard of soil by 270, that is, the number of cans filled per yard. If the soil costs you $19.00 per yard, your unit cost is about $.07 per gallon can.

The widest variety of nursery material is retailed in these containers. That a plant is sold in a gallon container does not mean that it has spent its whole life in that pot. Most of the material in gallons is transplanted from the liners, flats and plugs produced in Stage One.

The least expensive material to transplant into gallons is what you yourself generate in Stage One. However, if you have no desire to start at Stage One, preferring to eliminate any frustrations that go with methods of propagation you do not know or care to try, or if you cannot hold containerized stock through a frigid winter, invest in plants which someone else has produced. Buying material for transplanting opens a door to the full range of plant material that is grown.

HOW DO YOU FIND SOURCES FOR PLANTS?

If your only experience with nurseries to this point has been with retail stores, then your first concern is how to find a wholesale grower. You might start by looking in the phone book under wholesale nurseries, but this will give you listings only for your immediate area. You can more readily find out who grows what by obtaining a list of the licensed nurseries in your state. This list may be available for a fee from the same government agency which licensed you. Different lists vary in their information, but generally they tell you whether a nursery is wholesale or retail and what broad categories of plants are grown by each.

Various state nurserymen associations have directories of their members. One of the best source materials available is the Directory and Buyers Guide from the Oregon Association of Nurserymen. The most important section is the Buyers Guide which contains listings for more than 20,000 plants, products and services. The plant list is divided into thirteen sections with the plants listed alphabetically in each section by botanical name. Various growers and their phone numbers are listed under each plant heading, which is further divided to tell you whether the grower sells the plants as liners, seedlings, bareroot, balled and burlapped, or container stock. Some growers have also placed individual ads indicating their specialties. Other states' nurserymen associations publish separate Buyers Guides which are most helpful in finding sources for plant material and supplies. Nurserymen associations of the United States and Canada are listed in Appendix One.

Trade shows are sponsored by nurserymen associations and they will be happy to tell you when and where one is being held near you. Wholesale growers, as well as distributors of nursery supplies and plant brokers, attend these shows. Plant brokers often represent a number of different growers from different states and foreign countries. Trade magazines carrying advertisements for many different growers are other sources of information.

Wholesale sources are even found by visiting retail nurseries. When you see plants in retail stores which you would like to buy for transplanting, look at the labels. Many growers include their name and address on the label. Even if it is just the company name, you can find the address in the license directory. Actually seeing a grower's product in a store allows you to make judgments about what you want to buy and what to expect if you order plants from him. Catalogues allow you to compare prices, but you cannot compare quality until you see the plants.

Retail stores themselves can be good sources for plants in cell packs, four-inch and gallons for shifting into larger containers and sometimes the best bargains can be found there. On one occasion we purchased a block of 100 gallon azaleas from a wholesaler at a cost of $2.05 each. We had checked around and the next lowest price we found was $2.29. One week after we took delivery we opened up the newspaper to find an ad from a home improvement center offering azaleas at $1.88. That was retail! What did they look like? We were curious about the quality, so we went to look them over. They looked just like ours. We looked at a label. The plants were from the same grower where we had gotten ours. By purchasing in the tens of thousands for all their stores, the chain store had gotten a much better price than we could ever get for just 100 plants. With almost no mark-up they were using the azaleas as an ad leader to attract business. They sure got our attention. Familiarize yourself with normal wholesale prices so that you can recognize these bargains when they come along. Another advantage to buying ad specials from discount stores is that you do not have to purchase minimum quantities or pay shipping. Some of the standard better buys from the discount retailers are the flowering bedding plants.

BEDDING PLANTS AND HERBACEOUS PERENNIALS

The market for larger annuals in gallon containers has been increasing over the years to the point of becoming a major part of the total sales. Annuals do not require much soil depth, so you can use shallow containers such as the 6" x 5" black plastic pots with a capacity of 119 cu. in. at a cost of only $.17 each. With a cubic yard of soil you can fill almost 400 of these cans, which are appropriately called 6" Scotch pots.

Bedding plants are sometimes planted in the round green or white plastic pots which are 6" in diameter, but shallow in depth. These pots can also be made into hanging baskets by drilling small holes in the rims of the pots and adding wire hangers. A twisted three-wire hanger costs $.12, a four-wire costs $.17, but you can sell a hanging basket for $1.00 to $2.00 more than the simple potted annual. More decorative styles of hanging baskets are also available from suppliers.

When planting gallon containers, transplant your seedlings or purchased plugs directly from the flats into the containers. Do not first transplant them into cell packs or four-inch pots and wait for them to grow larger to transplant again. If you are growing flowering bedding plants, use two to three plants per container. Multiple plants fill out the pot faster and make a more attractive presentation. Very few vegetables are transplanted into gallons, except tomatoes and peppers, and one to a container is fine.

Herbaceous flowering perennials propagated from seed and cuttings or purchased as plugs should be transplanted directly from the flats into gallon containers just as annuals, but one or two per container is sufficient for most perennials. As noted in Stage One, many herbaceous perennials do not naturally bloom their first year. In most cases, you cannot start from seed or cutting in the spring and expect to have a gallon size plant in bloom by the end of the growing season. To achieve marketable size in a short season, buy and transplant older seedlings, this means buying larger plugs or even using four-inch pots. The grower from whom you buy your plants can tell you which ones have been conditioned in order to bloom their first season in the gallon containers. Getting your gallon perennials to bloom is key to marketing. Many retailers want to buy gallon perennials only when they are budded and ready to bloom, for a perennial in bloom will sell itself.

A large number of perennials are cold hardy and can winter over in containers in many areas with little or no protection. In these areas, transplant perennials from smaller containers into gallons before winter in order to have plants ready for spring and summer blooming.

ORNAMENTAL SHRUBS, TREES AND VINES: LINERS

As noted earlier, very few shrubs, vines and trees are ever offered to the public in liner pots. The reason is simple, there is virtually no market. The public wants these plants in larger sizes and the smallest size that most people are willing to accept is the #1 or gallon container. The majority of ornamental plants are transplanted into gallons after being started elsewhere. There are nurseries which specialize in just propagating and selling liners to other growers. To these nurseries belong the frustrations of the unsuccessful cuttings, the seeds that never sprouted and the seedlings which were killed by fungus diseases. The buyer of liner material has been spared these disappointments and can transplant viable rooted plants into larger containers with considerably less worry of loss.

A plant grown in a liner pot has roots already established in soil. When the plant is removed from the pot, the soil should not be broken apart. There is no transplant shock if the roots remain undisturbed. This allows liner stock to be transplanted year-round; only the harshness of your own climate sets the limits on the planting season.

Prices for liners are generally between $.45 and $.70 each, but the smallest quantity in which you can order is by the flat count. Pricing may be by the 100 count with prices dropping at 500 and then again at 1,000. There can be problems with availability. Catalogues list plant varieties that are grown, but the plants will not always be available when you want them. Growers put out Availability Lists for what is ready for immediate sale. Many propagators grow only on a contract basis, doing very little on the speculation that someone will order what they have chosen to grow. To get what you want, plan ahead and order early. In many cases the growers ask for a 25% deposit before they begin to grow the plants.

Pricing in catalogues is FOB point of origin. Some nurseries ship liners on their own trucks and may waive shipping charges on minimum orders, but in most cases, growers ship via commercial carriers and not only is the shipping charged to you, but the additional costs for packing liners in shipping cartons is also charged to you. Most nurseries can ship liners directly to your door via UPS.

TRANSPLANTS FROM GROUND COVER FLATS

Almost any type of plant grown in ground cover flats can be transplanted directly into gallons, but for the majority of them this marks the end of the move-up line. Plants grown in ground cover flats are similar to liners in that they are rooted cuttings already growing in soil. However, they are not separated into individual pots. Separate the plants, keeping as much of the soil around the roots as possible. As noted earlier, cuttings propagated in ground cover flats cost only about $.08 to $.16 each. If minimum purchase requirements deter you from buying wholesale, watch for sales at the discount retailers. Flats are frequently advertised as leaders and are priced only cents above normal wholesale.

BAREROOT CUTTINGS

In Stage One we discussed how to make cuttings in flats filled with a rooting medium. If you have produced your own transplants in this way, you can shift them directly from the flats into the gallon containers without going through the liner stage. In the process of transplanting from propagating flats, you essentially bare root the plants for the short time they make the transition from the flat to the new container.

Cuttings removed from flats are not like fish out of water. They can be held out of soil for brief periods of time if care is taken that they not dry out. This allows producers to sell and ship evergreen cuttings in a bareroot state. The plants are removed from the flats and all the rooting medium is shaken off. They are then bundled or rolled in newspaper and packed in cartons with a small amount of moisture-holding sawdust or shredded newspaper covering the top. Since there is no container or soil involved, pricing of the bareroot cuttings is about 30 % less than liner stock.

Exposure to conditions which allow or accelerate drying of the roots and foliage is extremely dangerous for bareroot cuttings, so shipping is usually done in the coolest seasons of the year. The risk of losing bareroot evergreen cuttings is much greater than the risk of losing liner stock, especially if hot weather follows shortly after transplanting.

HANDLING BAREROOT MATERIAL

A great deal of nursery stock is sold in the bareroot state and it is important to know how to handle it upon delivery. Whether you are dealing with evergreen cuttings or with dormant deciduous plants, it is crucial that the roots, stems or foliage not be allowed to dry. Exposure to freezing temperatures must also be avoided. Bareroot material is packaged in bundles and, except for larger trees, is shipped in cartons. The cartons and the shipping are extra costs charged to the buyer. The first order of business upon delivery is to immediately open the cartons and inspect the material. Sometimes mildew has begun to develop and you need to get the plants out of the container right away. Cut the bundles open and get air circulation to the plants. If the plants are dry, either put the whole bundles in buckets filled with water or spray water over the plants. You must get the root systems covered as soon as possible. This does not mean that you begin to can the plants one by one at a feverish pace. Simply take the whole bundle, cut the strings tying it, separate it into smaller bundles or put the whole bundle into a regular nursery container with drainage holes. For the smallest plants use a gallon can, for the larger bundles use a five or fifteen gallon. Pour in soil around the roots and tamp it down. Use water pressure from a hose to wash soil into any air pockets. This will hold the cuttings for only a very short time. You should transplant them as soon as possible into their containers, because holding cuttings in bundles any extended period of time means that the plants on the inside are not receiving light or air and they can quickly begin to mildew. Evergreen cuttings should be transplanted into containers within a few days, but dormant material can be held much longer. But you do need to get your dormant bareroot material canned before the weather warms and the plants begin to put out their new white feeder roots. These roots are tender and easily torn causing transplant shock. Warmer weather is particularly hard on bareroot plants and hot weather will bring excessive loss. It is important that the plants begin to establish their roots in the soil while it is still cool. Remember that the soil in black plastic containers absorbs much more heat than the ground.

Most dormant bareroot begins to grow as the weather warms, but occasionally some plants need help waking up, especially if they have been in cold storage for a long time. You may have to put the bundles in a hothouse or cover the tops with plastic for a few days to force the buds to open. This is called sweating. If you are inexperienced with bareroot, do not be shy about asking the grower for advice on how to treat specific plants. Let's now take a look at some other types of bareroot material.

FOREST SEEDLINGS

The incredibly cheap price of forest seedlings, that is, conifers such as spruce, pine, cedar and fir, is an attractive lure to backyard growers looking to buy plants to grow and resell. One individual heard that he could buy two-year old Scotch pines for only $.19 each if he bought them in quantities of 1,000. That was an investment of only $190.00 and he saw the potential for a huge profit. So he ordered the trees, paid his money and waited patiently for the nursery to notify him that his order was ready. When that day came, he hitched up his trailer to his truck and got a friend with a second pickup to follow him to the nursery. He was at first bewildered and then grew red with embarrassment when he was handed one not-so-heavy cardboard box with all 1,000 seedlings inside.

This fellow was truly disappointed because the product he received did not match the picture he had developed in his mind. What should he have expected? A wide variety of conifers are grown from seed sown by machine into specially prepared beds out in the open fields. The seedlings are carefully tended one, two or three years until the onset of winter when the plants go into semi-dormancy and can be dug with minimal damage or risk to survival. The trees are then sorted and graded. Catalogues designate the different ages of the seedlings with two numbers separated by a hyphen, for example, 1-0 means that the seedling has been in the seed bed one year. The second number is the number of years it has spent in a transplant bed. A 1-0 seedling has spent one year in the seed bed and none in the transplant bed. After one or more years in a seed bed a tree may be dug up, receiving some root pruning in the process in order to encourage more fibrous root growth, and then be transplanted into another bed where it receives more room to grow. Such a seedling is designated by 1-1 for one year in the seed bed and one year in the transplant bed or 2-1 for two years in the seed bed and one year in the transplant bed. Adding the two figures together gives you the age of the seedling.

Some growers grade their seedlings both by age and by size. These catalogue listings give a much clearer idea what to expect in size. You can see from a description that a 2-0 Scotch pine may be only 3" to 12" after two years of growing. Most conifers grow rather slowly and, for the more impatient grower, the majority of the 1-0 or 2-0 forest seedlings do not make good candidates for container growing. The exceptions are cedars, redwoods and some varieties of pine which do grow quickly enough to reach marketable size in one season.

Table 4.2 Common bareroot conifer seedlings

abies	metasequoia	sequoia sempervirens
cedrus	picea	sequoiadendron
cupressus	pinus	taxodium
juniperus	pseudolarix	thuja
larix	pseudotsuga	tsuga

Conifers are usually priced by quantities of 100, 500 and 1,000. The major customers for conifer seedlings are growers who replant the seedlings in the ground where they take less maintenance, such as reforestation projects, Christmas tree farms and nurseries which produce balled and burlapped stock.

DECIDUOUS SHRUBS

A wide variety of ornamental broadleaf deciduous shrubs begin their lives in the specially prepared ground of nursery fields. Many are sown from seed, others are propagated from cuttings. When they go dormant in late fall and early winter, they are dug, sorted, graded, bundled and held in cold storage until shipped. They are sold and shipped bareroot through the winter months and into early spring. In warmer climates it is best to take delivery in January and February; June is the latest month for shipping to the coldest climates. Shrubs are graded by height alone or by age and height. Table 4.3 gives a typical catalogue listing for the common lilac.

Table 4.3 Common lilac bareroot seedling pricing

age	size	price/100	price/500	price/2,500
2-0	6-12"	$.39	$.26	$.23
2-0	12-18"	$.48	$.32	$.29
2-0	18-24"	$.57	$.38	$.35
3-0	12-18"	$.51	$.35	$.32
3-0	18-24"	$.63	$.42	$.38
3-0	2-3'	$.83	$.55	$.50

Most of the plants that bareroot seedling growers produce are grown for other nurserymen who replant them and grow them on to larger retail sizes. Much of the material is replanted in the ground and resold as larger bareroot or balled and burlapped stock. When transplanted into one gallon containers, the 1-0 and 2-0 material between 6" and 18", in 100 count bundles, is usually used. Bareroot offers excellent value to the nurseryman, since it is usually larger in height and root system than liners which cost more, and larger bareroot plants can fill out a gallon container in a shorter growing time. Ultimately the real test is what the plants look like when they arrive. You cannot recognize a true bargain until you have something to examine and compare. When you first start out dealing with seedling growers, buy minimum orders from several different sources and determine for yourself whose quality is best and whose service meets your needs.

Price is not the only factor that determines the best source. Quality and service are both worth extra money. For example, if one supplier cannot deliver until March, but in your climate the weather is already getting warm, and you do not have enough time to get everything canned before it gets too hot, buy from the grower who charges slightly more, but delivers in January.

TREES

Seedling trees sometimes are graded by height and by caliper, which is the diameter of the trunk measured at ground level. If trees are graded only by caliper, ask the grower if the trees have been topped. Some seedling trees are specifically grown to be rootstock for grafting and have the tops cut out in order to increase the caliper of the trunk for grafting purposes. The top of these seedlings is of no concern since it is cut away after grafting. If simply replanted as they are, topped seedlings have to regrow new central leaders which are likely to be crooked. If you are not grafting, buy trees which have not been topped. These trees should be fairly straight and should continue to grow that way. Trees graded by height alone usually have not been topped.

Outside of Japanese maples, few seedling trees are canned into one gallon containers for retail sale since there is very little public demand for small trees. Most gallon trees are grown to be shifted into #5s or larger containers. Table 4.4 lists some common field grown bareroot shrub and tree seedlings.

Table 4.4 Common field grown bareroot

acer	fagus	phellodendron
aesculus	forsythia	platanus
alnus	fraxinus	populus
amelanchier	ginkgo	potentilla
arctostaphylos	gleditsia	prunus
aronia	gymnocladus	pyrus
artemisia	hamamelis	quercus
berberis	hippophae	rhamnus
betula	koelreuteria	rhus
caragana	kolkwitzia	ribes
castanea	ligustrum	rosa
catalpa	liquidambar	salix
celtis	liriodendron	sambucus
cercidiphyllum	lithocarpus	sorbus
cercis	lonicera	spiraea
cornus	magnolia	syringa
corylus	mahonia	tilia
cotinus	malus	ulmus
cotoneaster	morus	viburnum
crataegus	nyssa sylvatica	weigela
elaeagnus	paulownia	wisteria

The profit potentials are very good when you know how to use bareroot material. But keep in mind that the seedling grower is selling wholesale to other professionals, and he does not guarantee your success. You purchase the plants without warranty as to viability and you have to expect and accept some loss in the transplanting.

PLANTING ONE GALLON CONTAINERS

The planting process is anything but technical, but if you can learn to do it wearing a pair of gloves you will avoid two problems: first, your hands will not have ground-in dirt that only goes away when you grow a fresh layer of skin, and secondly, you will avoid getting splinters in your hands and fingers from the compost. The planting method differs from that in Stage One only in that you use a bigger container. If you are using moist soil, fill the container to the top and form a hole in the soil with your hand or some kind of a punch, for example, a short piece of 2"x 2" wood makes a nice hole punch for liners. If you are using a time release fertilizer, you do not have to mix it into the soil, you can just put it in the hole and stir it around. Do not put it on the surface after planting. Time release fertilizer works when water breaks down the resin coating on the pellets, and it works best when the prill is completely covered by moistened soil. Insert your plant into the hole, then tamp down the soil leaving about an inch at the top for watering.

If your soil is too dry and you cannot get it sufficiently moistened to hold the shape of the hole you punch, fill the container about only one-half to two-thirds full. Add time release fertilizer. Position your liner so that its soil line or highest root is about 1 1/2" below the rim of the can, add the rest of the soil and tamp down.

When transplanting bareroot seedlings with larger root systems, take your plant in one hand and hold it in the center of an empty one gallon can, keeping the highest root approximately 1" to 1 1/2" below the rim of the can. With another empty gallon container, scoop up a can of soil and pour it around the seedling. Fill the can only two-thirds full and add your fertilizer to the soil. Then fill the container to the top and tamp down. It is not at all exhausting to do fifty or more gallon containers in an hour. The most important step after planting is watering. It takes several applications of water before the dirt has absorbed enough to actually be moist around the roots. Plan on watering your newly planted containers three to five times until they are thoroughly moistened.

CHAPTER 5

STAGE THREE: THE PRODUCTION OF TWO, THREE AND FOUR GALLONS

This stage of production deals with containers in the mid-sizes between one and five gallons. Annuals are able to grow fast enough to go from seed to marketable plants in these containers within a single growing season, but if you are propagating your own perennial shrubs, trees and vines for transplanting into two, three or four gallons, you will have to hold most species through a winter season and sell them in the next year. To produce marketable perennial plants in these containers within a single growing season, you must start with larger transplants in the spring. These may be starter plants which you wintered over from the previous season or plants bought from another grower.

As the capacity of the containers increases, so does the weight factor of the canned plant: a planted #2 weighs about ten to twelve lbs., a #3 about sixteen to twenty lbs., a #4 about twenty-two to twenty-five lbs. To calculate your costs for soil and fertilizer you need only multiply the cost for a #1 by the size of the larger container. If it takes $.14 worth of soil and fertilizer for a #1 can, it takes about $.28 for a #2, $.42 for a #3, and $.56 for a #4. This is not precise, since capacities vary between types, but it works for a reasonable estimate.

Pricing and capacity of several different types of containers are given in Table 5.1. The availability of used #2s, #3s and #4s is much more limited than used #1s. Commercial landscaping projects seldom call for plants in sizes other than #1s, #5s and #15s. The greatest portion of plants in the mid-sizes is retailed to the homeowner who usually throws the cans away one at a time.

Table 5.1 Two, three and four gallon containers

type of pot	size	capacity	# per case	unit price
black plastic	# 2	403 cu. in.	50	$.39
blow molded	# 2	370 cu. in.	50	$.34
pulp fiber	8" x 8"	346 cu. in.	72	$.42
black plastic	#3	665 cu. in.	50	$.66
blow molded	#3	658 cu. in.	50	$.44
pulp fiber	12" x 8"	606 cu. in.	44	$.81
black plastic	#4	952 cu. in.	25	$.90
blow molded	#4	785 cu. in.	25	$.67
pulp fiber	12" x 11"	812 cu. in.	32	$.89

Nursery plants do not go through an exact numerical progression being transferred from flat to liner to #1s into #2s, then into #3s and so on. Much nursery stock is transplanted only once or twice to reach this stage of production and for many plants this stage marks the end of the production line.

COLOR POTS, BOWLS AND BASKETS

Different annuals are not intermixed in the cell packs and pots in Stages One and Two. You may continue in this same vein in this stage of production, but the expanded planting areas of larger containers offer you a wonderful opportunity to branch out and to mix different annuals together. Your gardening talents are free to blossom in Stage Three by creating mini-flower gardens.

Two and three gallon containers planted with mixtures of different flowering annuals are called color pots and their bright and varied display of flowers is a dependable seller. The molded pulp pots tend to be used more frequently than plastic containers since the manufacturers have developed a patio planter series well suited to the purpose. One of the most popular sizes is the 15" wide by 6" deep bowl which costs about $1.12 each in forty count cases. Terra cotta colored plastic bowls are also available in a 12" wide by 5" deep size for $1.60 and a 14" wide by 5 1/4" deep bowl for $1.85.

Color pots and bowls are a viable option for the backyard grower who likes annuals but does not have the climate modification necessary to germinate seed and promote early growth. Wait until the freezing weather is past and then buy your bedding plants in six-packs, either from a wholesaler or the discount retailers. This frees you from growing plants from seed or pre-ordering plugs, and it allows you to select from a wide variety of plants which you can purchase in small quantities.

Select plants that appeal to you and mix two, three or four different types together keeping an eye to color. Be careful not to mix shade plants with sun plants. Not everything has to be a flowering plant. The combination of coleus, grown for its leaf colors, and impatiens, grown for flowers, makes a very attractive presentation. Different textures and color combinations create interest and appeal. It is fun putting things together and seeing how they look and how they sell. Experiment and enjoy.

The popular 15" pulp fiber bowl has a two and one-half gallon capacity, so it takes about $.35 worth of soil and fertilizer to fill it. Using eight to ten plants from the cell packs, which cost about $.16 each from discount retailers, the finished cost is under $3.00 for each bowl. This can easily be reduced with a little careful buying. On one May day while visiting the farmers market, we watched one grower virtually sell out of the fifty color bowls he had brought, and each one was priced at $10.00.

Bedding plants arranged in color bowls.

If you are growing in pulp pots, take care not to allow them to sit in water or mud. The pots are biodegradable and standing in water speeds the process along. Wooden pallets are an option to using tables or graveling the area. Shade cloth overhead is also useful for protecting the color pots from excessive sun and drying.

Patio pots are designed for placement on a flat surface, but many a patio is graced by colorful annuals in hanging baskets. Most anything grown in the patio pots works in baskets, although it is nice to use some plants with spreading habits which trail over the sides. You can grow the baskets on the ground like any other containers. Simply add the hanger at the time of sale; or you can make special provision to hang the containers while they are growing and thereby increase your production space by leaving room for something else on the ground. Pricing for some hanging baskets including the wire hangers is given in Table 5.2.

Since there is less surface area in the hanging baskets, they are more frequently filled with plants of the same species rather than mixing varieties as in the bowls, but that is really no reason to stifle your creativity. Continue to be innovative and see what develops. If something does not work, dump out the failures and replant. Hanging baskets are no harder to grow than any other color pot, but they bring a higher selling price because of their more decorative presentation.

Table 5.2 Hanging Baskets

type	width	depth	price each
plastic	7 1/2"	4 3/4"	$.29
plastic	9 1/2"	5"	$.58
plastic	10"	5 3/4"	$.75
plastic	12"	6 3/4"	$1.75
pulp	8" square	n/a	$.95
pulp	10" round	n/a	$1.20
pulp	12" round	n/a	$1.54

For all practical purposes the color pots, bowls and baskets mark the end of the move-up line for bedding plants and we end our discussion of annuals here.

HERBACEOUS PERENNIALS

Stage three also marks the end of the move up line for most of the herbaceous perennials. Many perennials must be started by fall and wintered over in order to be mature enough to bloom in the next year. If you cannot start your plants from seed early, buy plants in three or four-inch pots or use larger bareroot perennials propagated by division. Transplant in late winter or early spring. Two gallon perennials are extremely slow sellers when they are not flowering, so the goal is to bring them into bloom within the growing season. Timing is difficult even with one gallon perennials, and when you put them in two gallons you are asking more from the plants. Experiment with market timing, for it will vary with different plants. It does not take twice the time to produce a two gallon plant as a one gallon, nor must the plant be twice the size. If you transplant two plants of the same size, putting one into a one gallon and the other into a two gallon, the #2 will outgrow the #1 in the same time span. The two gallon has more soil in which the plant can develop a larger root system, which in turn allows the plant to absorb more nutrients from the extra fertilizer in the soil, thereby producing more rapid growth. And as far as size is concerned, just by virtue of being in the larger container a two gallon plant looks bigger than a one gallon.

Instead of starting out in the spring to grow a two gallon crop of perennials, it may be better to concentrate on growing perennials in cell packs, four-inch pots and gallon cans since it is not likely that you can get the plants to two gallon size before the blooming season passes. At the end of the selling season, if you are able to winter over perennial material, transplant any unmarketed plants into two gallons. Transplanting reinvigorates the plants so that they look fresh again in the spring and are ready to bloom in their proper season. If you still have two gallon perennials left over at the end of the selling season, divide them into smaller plants, make cuttings or plant them in the ground to use for division or cuttings in the spring.

Color pots and bowls are less frequently created from perennials because many do not bloom in their first year. Many more have much shorter blooming seasons than annuals and are not attractive in bowls when out of color. Choose plants which will remain in bloom for extended periods. For example, use a zonal geranium as the center piece and arrange smaller annuals around it.

A number of perennials make attractive hanging baskets, such as ivy geraniums, trailing lantana, fuchsias and tuberous begonias. Plant two to three to a container so that they fill out the basket more quickly and give it a balanced look.

WOODY ORNAMENTAL SHRUBS

In theory, any of the ornamental shrubs grown in the earlier stages can be transplanted into the mid-size containers. In practice, some smaller shrubs reach the end of their move up line in #2 containers, but most shrubs are planted into one gallons and five gallons, not into #2s, #3s and #4s. Why? Basically, there is no need to have plants in every size container, nor is there enough room in the retail stores to carry all the different sizes. The industry tends to standardize. Read catalogues to see what is grown and visit retail nurseries to see what is carried.

Most of the shrubs and vines grown in two gallons are transplanted from liners, such as azaleas and rhododendrons, or from bareroot such as lilacs and grapes. Bareroot plants can be purchased already grown to marketable size for #2, #3 and #4 containers, but few liner plants grow quickly enough to go from liner to two gallon size in a nine month growing season. Either transplant fast growing liner varieties which can reach marketable size while there is still time in the selling season or be prepared to carry the material through a winter. In climates where broadleaf evergreen shrubs are grown, the plants weather the winter in containers with little or no additional protection. The more cold tolerant the shrub, the less worry of its freezing to death over the winter.

The blooming season is beneficial but not crucial to marketing shrubs. When customers begin to look at plants in containers larger than one gallons, the size of the plant becomes more important than a flower on the plant. Basic landscape shrubs continue to sell throughout the year, but picture tags become useful sales tools for marketing plants out of bloom.

There is market potential for both blooming and non-blooming ornamentals in the mid-sizes, but before you create an entire crop in these sizes, research the market. What are the prospects of selling plants to nurseries in odd sized containers? Will you be able to get the higher price for the larger container? And always remember, just because a market does not currently exist, it does not mean that you cannot create one with the right product. There are a lot of opportunities waiting to be tapped. Let's consider some of the bareroot resources.

ROSES

The most common bareroot plants canned into two or three gallon containers are roses. All types can be easily propagated from cuttings. Miniature roses are usually greenhouse grown in small pots. Old fashioned roses, which are more difficult to find, are frequently propagated from cuttings planted right in the container. Rugosa types, which are extremely popular in the coldest climates, are field grown from seeds or cuttings and may be graded like other bareroot seedlings by age and height. Sometimes the number of canes is given. The best values on these rugosa types are found from the seedling growers. For example, a 1-0 "F. J. Grootendorst" bareroot rogusa rose wholesales for $.53 in quantities of 100. Transplanted in the late winter or early spring into #2 containers they can quickly reach marketable size in two to four months. The profit potential is excellent as shown by one wholesale catalogue which lists "F. J. Grootendorst" roses in #2 containers at $8.00.

The hybrid tea, floribunda, grandiflora and climbing roses, although they can be rooted from their canes directly in containers, are commercially propagated in fields and are grafted in a process called T-budding. A grower plants his field with the rootstock variety and later buds onto it the different hybrid varieties. The rootstock has a root system that can tolerate greater cold conditions and is less susceptible to nematodes, but the real value of the rootstock is its vigor. Some of the hybrid varieties, especially lavenders and yellows, are not vigorous growers on their own roots and do not produce the large flowers that customers have come to expect. This makes hybrid roses which are not T-budded less commercially valuable to the retail nurseries.

Field grown roses remain in the ground until the onset of cooler weather in November or December. As they go into dormancy they are dug from the ground, sorted, graded and then tied into bundles of ten. The bundles are heeled into holding beds of sawdust or sand, or in other cases held in cold storage until shipped. A true bareroot is boxed and shipped with nothing around its roots. When you take delivery, you must immediately heel the bundles into a holding bed or container.

Roses commonly used to be sold by retail nurseries as bareroot plants lined out in rows in sawdust or sand beds. When a customer selected one, it was pulled out and wrapped for the customer to take home. This method of sale has become so rare that most people now think that a bareroot rose only

106

comes in a plastic bag. A pretty picture of the flower on the package shows you what to expect in just a few short months. This packaging, which adds $.75 or more to the wholesale price, is used for the ease of marketing and adds nothing at all to the worth of the plant. The retailer has only to unpack the carton and set out the bagged roses in a display. He does not have to heel them into compost or pull them out and wrap them for the customer. And that pretty picture helps sell a plant that is otherwise only a bundle of thorny canes. But all the packaging goes into the garbage when the rose is planted. Do not pay extra for packaging you do not need and which requires the extra work of removing each rose from the plastic bag. You can save the packaging costs and time by ordering true bareroots. Orders need to be placed in advance to be sure of getting the varieties you want.

There are two major categories of hybrid grafted roses: patented and non-patented. Roses are probably the most highly worked area of new ornamental plant development. People look forward to the new roses every year. New varieties are protected by the patent laws and each plant has a premium added to the cost in order to pay the royalty to the developer. Patented roses always cost more. Non-patented roses are usually the older favorites whose patent life has run out and require no royalty payments and are, therefore, less expensive. There is little or no difference in quality of the roses. Most of the non-patented roses were award winning beauties when they made their debut and their beauty has not faded over the years. Our years of selling roses has taught us one thing: a rose in bloom has its own bewitching attraction that makes the name insignificant, patented or non-patented.

There are three grades for patented and non-patented bareroot roses: #1, #1 1/2 and #2. This grading applies only to budded roses. Roses on their own rootstock are not graded on this standard. These grades have nothing to do with the health of the plant and only little to do with its viability, but rather are used to grade size. A #1 rose must have three or more canes starting within three inches of the bud graft, and two of them must be at least 18" long; a #1 1/2 must have two canes or more which are 15" long, and a #2 should have two canes. This grading is on plants as they come from the field and frequently growers cut the canes shorter for shipping or canning. All should be healthy roses.

In the field, one rose may overgrow another and shut out its light or soak up its nutrients, thereby slowing the other's growth. Once in a container the lower grade roses will not suffer the same competition and what you bought as a #1 1/2 will quickly put on new canes in a matter of a few weeks. If it is your intention to sell the roses bareroot, then a #1 makes a much better first impression than the lower grade and it will sell for more. However, once the containerized roses start to grow the distinctions vanish and you can sell the #1 1/2 for as much as the #1. The #1 1/2 may only need a few weeks more of growing time to make a very respectable rose. Therefore, in determining what grade to buy, time is a factor to consider. If you hope to turn the product quickly, the larger plant will be more immediately marketable, but the lower priced #1 1/2 will yield the greater profit for only a slightly longer growing period.

When the rose bush is dug from the field, you have a finished plant, fully developed and ready for transplanting into the garden. Yet, there are thousands of people who realize that when it comes to handling bareroot material, they have a black thumb. They prefer to buy roses leafed and blooming, that is, plants they know are alive. But even with a black thumb, there is nothing to putting a rose into a container.

First, put on a pair of gloves. Bareroot roses do much better if their long canes are shortened to a 6" or 8" length. Do your pruning before you containerize. Position the rose in the center of your empty container. Prune roots if necessary. Make sure that the highest root on the plant will be below the soil line and that any graft is above the soil. Shovel in soil to a level about two-thirds full. Add your time release fertilizer (roses are heavy feeders), tamp down, and fill the container to the top with more soil. Tamp down again, leaving the soil level at least an inch below the rim. Label your roses immediately or you will not know what you have later.

Bareroot rose canned
into a biodegradable
pulp pot, ready for im-
mediate sale.

If canning roses for resale is something you want to try but you are reluctant to place the minimum order necessary to buy from a wholesaler, there is another option. Sometimes the discount stores put the packaged, non-patented #1 1/2 roses on sale as loss leaders. For three years in a row, we have seen them advertised for $1.97, a price which leaves plenty of room for turning a profit when you containerize them in two gallons. You can buy just a few or several dozen. A good reason to take advantage of these sales is that many discount stores give unconditional guarantees on their plants, whereas a wholesaler gives no guarantee on viability.

BAREROOT SEEDLINGS:
CONIFERS AND WOODY ORNAMENTALS

We noted in Stage Two that few varieties of conifer seedlings in the 1-0 or 2-0 range make good one gallon backyard nursery crops. The plants are slow and the market is small. The older transplanted seedlings designated 2-1 or 2-2 represent a step up in bareroot size. They have more fibrous root systems because of root pruning, and they have heavier, more balanced top growth because they are transplanted further apart. A grower sells 15-18" (3-2) blue spruce seedlings in quantities of 100 for $1.35 each; the 18-24" (2-3) seedlings cost $2.40. These five year-old plants are already two gallon size and only need to be containerized. They need little or no extra growing time and can be offered for sale quickly at double the price you paid for the plant and the canning. The person who grew the tree from seed and waited five years gets $1.35 to $2.40 per plant; the nurseryman who buys the tree, takes a minute to put it in a container and holds it a short time until sale, can make the same amount within weeks or a few months. A backyard grower cannot afford the time and does not have the space to grow the hundreds of thousands of seedlings that make it profitable for the bareroot seedling growers. It is not to your advantage to spend extra years growing when you can buy a year's growing time for pennies. This is particularly true with conifers which grow slowly in their first two years and somewhat faster thereafter, but the same principle also applies to other field grown, deciduous ornamental seedlings.

There is a noticeable difference in size between bareroot and liner grown seedlings. The bareroot tree on the left cost $.40, the liner in the middle cost $.50, the bareroot on the right cost $.45.

Bareroot grading by size allows you to match the plant to the container and the closer you get to the size of a finished plant for a particular container size, the shorter the growing time to marketability. In other words, you can start with the smaller, cheaper plants and grow them on to the right size, or you can buy plants already at the marketable size and simply containerize them. For example, bareroot 6-12" (2-0) common purple lilacs sell for $.40 each in quantities of 100 and 18-24" (2-1) lilacs sell for $.65. For only a quarter more you can buy the three-year old transplant which has already grown a larger root system and six to twelve inches more top growth. Are you willing to spend an extra year growing a plant to that size for only a quarter?

Remember, you are not selling just a plant, you are selling time. Say a plant needs three years of growing time to go from seed to a two gallon plant worth $6.00. This means that the plant increases in value at the rate of $1.00 every six months. If you can purchase the first 2 1/2 years of your growing time for $.65, it makes the last six months you spend growing the plant worth $5.35. It does not profit you to grow the plant right from the beginning when you can buy that time so cheaply from another grower.

BIODEGRADABLE MOLDED PULP POTS

In our discussion of bareroot plants, we have seen that many different shrubs can be purchased in sizes which, when canned into the mid-sized containers, are immediately at marketable size. However, it takes time for roots to expand into the new soil and to develop a rootball which will hold together when the plant is removed from the container. If the plant is removed too early, the soil will break apart, tearing away the tender new feeder roots. This causes transplant shock which sets the plant back or may even result in death. The industry's solution to this problem is to containerize bareroot material into biodegradable pulp pots. The plant does not have to be removed from the container and instead can be transplanted container and all. The pulp fiber decomposes in the ground and roots grow through the pot. This means that no matter where the bareroot transplant is in its root development, it can be sold, taken home and planted, container and all, without suffering any transplant shock, since its roots are never disturbed. You have a marketable product as soon as you have planted it into the container, which explains why so many retail nurseries have roses in pulp pots.

Pulp pots are best for bareroot transplants which you do not intend to hold for long periods in the container. Remember, the pots are designed to biodegrade and the water which the plant needs is the key factor working to break down the pots. They will last longer if you keep them out of standing water and mud. Because of their biodegradable nature, you do not find these containers on the used market, so be sure to order containers early enough for delivery prior to your bareroot order's arrival. Pre-season discounts are also available on early orders. Table 5.3 gives pulp pot sizes suggested for bareroot.

Table 5.3 Pulp pots for bareroot

Size by height	Container size
12-15"	7" x 7" or 7" x 9"
15-18"	8" x 6" or 8" x 8"
18-24"	9" x 9" or 10" x 7"
2-3'	10" x10" or 12" x 8"
3-4'	12" x11" or 13" x 9"
4-5'	13" x12" or 15" x10"
5-6'	15" x13" or 15" x16"
6-8'	18" x12" or 18" x16"
roses	10" x10" or 12" x11"
Size by caliper	**Container size**
1/2 to 5/8"	12" x 11"
5/8 to 3/4"	13" x 12"
3/4 to 1 1/4"	15" x 13"
1 1/4 to 1 1/2"	15" x 16"
1 1/2 to 2"	18" x 16"

CHAPTER 6

STAGE FOUR: THE PRODUCTION OF FIVE GALLON PLANTS

In this stage of production we are basically dealing with shrubs, vines and trees. Most shrubs and vines retailed in one gallon containers are also sold in fives, but most varieties of trees are not retailed until they reach this stage of production. The desire on the part of homeowners to create an instant landscape with large plants has led to a boom in sales of five gallon material. Demand for larger plants has also been fueled by city and county planning departments which require that developers use large numbers of fives in their landscaping of new apartments, offices and shopping centers. High consumer demand and a selling price over three times more than a one gallon make this stage of production potentially one of the most profitable for the backyard grower. However, you must note that planted five gallon containers which weigh between twenty-five and thirty lbs. also make greater demands on your back.

In Table 6.1 compare the price and capacity of three types of #5 containers.

Table 6.1   #5 Containers

type of pot	width	depth	capacity	# per case	unit price
black plastic	12"	9"	952 cu.in.	20	$1.47
blow molded	12"	11 1/4"	945 cu.in.	50	$0.89
pulp	13"	9"	956 cu.in.	40	$0.99

There is a substantial savings in using the blow molded containers instead of the regular black plastic. When the thinner blow molded plastic pots first appeared on the market, we were scornful of their lightweight fabrication, but we gained respect for them when we found that we could step on them and then simply pound them back into shape. The regular cans, when stepped on, are likely to split and become unusable.

Types of blow molded pots.

Five gallon containers are so widely planted that used pots are fairly easy to find from nurseries and landscapers. We never buy new #5 containers since we always find a good supply of used at $.20 or $.25 each. If you can find used fives for $.25, your canning cost for all your components of can, soil and fertilizer is under $.90 a unit. Availability and demand in your area may increase what you have to pay.

SHIFTING SMALLER CONTAINER MATERIAL

It takes a plant two to three years growing time to go from seed or cutting to marketable five gallon size. In climates where nature allows this process to proceed without need for special winter protection, you can consider starting with liner pots.

By planting liners directly into five gallons, you skip the intermediate step of growing the plant through the gallon stage. The cost advantage is obvious; a liner costs between $.50 and $.75 while a gallon costs between $2.00 and $3.00. Despite the price differential, planting liners directly into fives is not widely practiced in the nursery industry. Most growers prefer to transplant the liner into a gallon first. This gives them the option of selling that plant when it has reached the stage of a marketable gallon. If it does not sell and continues to grow larger, they have the option of transplanting it into the five gallon. By cutting out the gallon stage you save a few minutes of planting time, but are committed to waiting until the plant gets to five gallon size before you are able to market it.

On the other hand, we noted earlier that a plant grows at a faster rate when it has more soil and fertilizer available in the container. If you start your liner in a five you cannot sell it when it reaches the one gallon size, but you can expect it to reach five gallon size somewhat sooner than it would if it went from liner to gallon to five gallon. This holds true especially for the faster growing plants; but if you are relying on time release fertilizer to feed the plant, it may run out of food before it has reached the marketable size and will require additional fertilizer. Should you fail to heed the plant's need for additional food, you will find that the plant will fail to reach your expectations. This becomes most obvious with slower growing plants. Determining which liners will work best for you is a process of trial and error based on the unique conditions of your own operation. You really lose nothing by experimenting with small numbers.

Since trees are not usually retailed in one gallons, they are more frequently transplanted from liners into fives, especially from the 7" to 10" deep tree pots and bands. Although only 2" to 2 1/2" wide, these liners are as deep as gallon cans and transplant nicely into fives.

Most plants in fives are shifted up from ones rather than liners. If you buy shifting material from another grower, there are two ways you can go. You can make a list of what you want to grow and then buy it at the catalogue prices listed, or you can let sale prices determine what you grow. If you are going to be a bargain shopper, you have to be open to a process of random selection based on the best bargain. Market conditions may force a reduction in price on one variety of plant one year and something else the next year; every season brings some kind of bargain, but not the same ones year-to-year. To find what wholesale nurseries have on sale, you have to be on their mailing lists or make contact with their salespeople. And remember to check the sales at retail stores.

You must avoid getting carried away with what appears to be a great bargain. Sometimes growers are anxious to sell winter sensitive stock in the fall before a harsh and unpredictable winter can seriously damage and kill material that they cannot protect. If you too are unable to protect such material, then these plants are no bargain for you at any price. In fact, you should be thinking about liquidating any such plants that you are holding.

We are most accustomed to think of bargains in terms of price, but in a business selling time, you must also consider the time factor involved in growing. It takes time to grow a plant to a larger size. Liners tend to be somewhat uniform in size and age, but this is not the case with plants in gallons. If a crop of ones fails to sell out after it reaches marketability, the plants still continue growing to larger sizes. For example, a plant may become marketable at 10" high, but it does not stop growing and may double in height before it sells. Since catalogue prices are by size of the container, not size of the plant, a grower nets nothing extra for the larger plant still in a gallon container. These plants are said to be overgrown, and nurseries prefer to use the largest one gallons for transplanting into fives. When you find such overgrown gallons for sale, you have an excellent opportunity to save yourself time in the production of your fives. This applies, of course, to any of the overgrown plants you yourself have in gallons.

The #5 on the left is a newly shifted overgrown #1 nandina like the #1 on the right. The center plant is a standard marketable #1 nandina.

Many times the overgrown gallon looks like a five as soon as it is shifted. Unfortunately, oftentimes a nursery sells these plants before they have had time to root out completely in their new containers. Too many people have taken a five gallon plant home and, upon removing it from the container, have watched all the soil drop off exposing the rootball of a gallon size plant. They are right to resent paying a five gallon price for a one gallon plant. For the higher price the customer does deserve the root system of the five gallon plant, not just the appearance. Therefore, plants shifted up from plastic containers are usually not transplanted into pulp pots for immediate sale, but continue to be grown in plastic and given time to develop the larger root system. A few extra months may be all that is needed.

In the warmer climates, liners and ones can be transplanted into fives at any time of the year without problems. It seems, however, that many gardeners have heard that at the time of transplanting they should break up the rootball so that the plant's roots are better able to spread and do not circle. This advice is given indiscriminately. Many plants are lost unnecessarily when their rootballs are torn apart by well-intentioned gardeners. This is especially true in hot weather. Only a very root bound plant needs its rootball broken up. Inspect your rootball to see its condition. Roots right on the soil's edge are absolutely normal and do not mean that the plant is root bound. Roots typically go to the edge of the can first. Most nursery stock from wholesalers is not root bound; to break-up the rootball is unnecessary on fresh material and only causes trauma that may result in damage or death.

To transplant a #1 into a #5 is simple. Fill your container about half full with soil, position the plant so that its soil level is about one inch below the rim of the #5, add your time release fertilizer and fill in with soil. A particularly useful tool for canning five gallon material is a two to three foot long 2" x 2" piece of wood. Use it to tamp down the soil. It saves a lot of bending. The stick is also perfect for separating used containers which landscapers have jammed so tightly inside one another that you cannot pull them apart. By tapping, and sometimes really whapping along the top rim, you can knock the containers loose. You can generally containerize and move into your holding area about twenty-five to thirty #5 containers per hour.

There are two side benefits in transplanting ones into fives. First, you get a small rebate on the purchase price of the plant with the empty one gallon container which you can re-use. Secondly, since the one gallon plant already has a gallon size rootball, you need only four gallons of new soil. This reduces your soil cost for a five by about $.07. The savings are small per plant, but become significant when you are doing large numbers.

Tamping down the soil around a transplant with a 2" x 2" stick.

PATENTED MATERIAL

Buying gallon plants for shifting opens another door to you formerly closed because of patent laws. You can purchase patented gallon plants and bareroots from growers who have paid the patent fees and have the right to propagate them. In some cases patented liners are available, but many growers prefer to plant them into gallons and get the higher price for themselves. The patent fee is passed on to you in the price of the plant. When buying patented plants, make sure that the patent tag is either on the plant or included separately in the shipment. The patent tag must be on the plant when you resell it.

There is no patent infringement when you transfer one of these plants into a five gallon container. You are not reproducing the plant, just transplanting it into a larger container. This opens up a wider market for the specialty plants which are more in fashion in landscaping. Since the common plants are offered so widely at cheaper prices in the discount stores, many of the full service nurseries are going more toward the higher end market which means carrying more patented specialty plants. Check the catalogue prices in order to determine what your profit margin can be for just transferring ones to fives.

BAREROOT

Many varieties of bareroot deciduous shrubs, vines and trees are transplanted into fives during the winter and early spring. Transplanting bareroot is quite easy. With one hand hold the plant in the center of an empty #5 so that the highest root is about 1 1/2" to 2" below the rim. Shovel in soil to about two-thirds full, add time release fertilizer and tamp down. Fill to the top and tamp down again leaving about an inch space at the top for watering. There are two types of bareroot which you can work with in this stage: seedlings and retail-ready bareroot. We noted earlier that bareroot seedlings are not grown to be a finished retail product, but are sold to other growers who replant them and grow them on to larger retail sizes or use them for grafting rootstocks. For canning into five gallons, it is much more difficult to find seedlings which have grown large enough to be at a marketable size when transplanted. Most seedlings require additional growing time to reach five gallon size. How much time depends on the size of the plant you start with and its rate of growth. This is where it helps if you can read between the lines of catalogue listings. If you pay attention to the relationship between the two factors of age and height, you can get a very good idea what kind of growth rate you can expect from any of the seedlings graded by age and size. Consider what table 6.2 tells you about blue spruce and birch trees.

Table 6.2

BLUE SPRUCE		EUROPEAN WHITE BIRCH	
age	height	age	height
2-0	3-6"	2-0	6-12"
2-0	6-9"	2-0	12-18"
2-0	9-12"	2-0	18-24"
3-0	12-15"	2-0	2-3'
2-3	15-18"	2-0	3-4'
2-3	18-24"	2-0	4-5'

The grading reveals that the largest size the grower expects a two-year old blue spruce to reach is twelve inches, his three-year old spruce will grow to fifteen inches and his five-year old plant, which spends two years in the seed bed and three additional years in a transplant bed, is expected to attain only twenty-four inches. Clearly the blue spruce is a slow growing plant. On the other hand, the European white birch can be expected to reach a height of five feet in only two years. Knowing what growth is possible from a plant helps you to determine which size you want to transplant into a five gallon. If the plant is slow growing, start with the larger, older seedlings. When the plant is fast growing you can start with smaller, less expensive seedlings and still expect them to reach a good size in the growing season.

Occasionally, bareroot seedlings grow to sizes which overlap into the range of larger retail-ready bareroot. One season, a seedling nursery listed 2-3' (2-2) lilacs at $1.67 and 3-4' (2-2) lilacs at $2.12. These four year-old plants had grown to the sizes of retail-ready bareroot which sells at much higher prices. For example, another catalogue listed the 2-3' retail-ready bare root lilacs at $5.00 and the 3-4' at $6.20. A seedling grower may only have such large sizes available in years when he failed to sell the crop of smaller sizes the previous year and has been forced to leave plants in the field another year, or to replant what had been dug but did not sell. These plants correspond to overgrown container stock. When there are opportunities to buy such large seedlings, the savings over retail-ready bareroot prices translate to more profit for you.

Since most retail nurseries do not deal with seedling growers, but rather the growers and distributors of the larger retail-ready bareroot, we have been able to realize some immediate profits on overgrown seedlings by reselling them to retailers for about 25% below retail-ready bareroot prices. This is a bargain for the retailer, compared to the price he is used to paying, and we more than double our money for just handling the plants.

Research catalogues to find the best values for the current year. Quantities of larger seedlings are limited, so order early. Growers can only project how big they expect the plants to be by the end of the growing season. Due to the fickleness of nature, there are no guarantees that you will get the size you order, so specify the minimum size that you are willing to accept.

To this point, we have been dealing with bareroot products grown by seedling nurseries, but now it is time to consider those nurseries which have grown the seedlings on to larger sizes or grafted new varieties onto the seedling rootstocks. These growers specialize in retail-ready material.

Larger retail-ready bareroots are graded by height and caliper, with no notation given for age. Table 6.3 gives a catalogue listing for European white birch.

Table 6.3 European white birch

caliper	height	@ per 10	@ per 100
3/8"	3-4'	$4.95	$4.65
1/2"	4-5'	$5.90	$5.50
5/8"	5-6'	$7.00	$6.70
3/4"	6-8'	$8.10	$7.70

The caliper of the trunk is not measured at the root crown as on the small seedlings but about two inches above the ground line. One of the first things to notice with larger bareroot is that the pricing increments are much greater between sizes than with seedling trees. The pricing difference is in dollars not cents. There is another difference as well. Since bareroots have no container, they are priced by the size of the plant. Containerized material, on the other hand, is priced by the size of the container, not the size of the plant. A normal size range for five gallon birch trees is 5/8" to 3/4" in caliper and six to eight feet in height. Now, whether you put a 5/8" bareroot costing $7.00 or a 3/4" costing $8.10 into a five gallon, the act of containerizing them equalizes the price and both trees will sell for the same amount once in the can.

Much of the retail-ready bareroot is grafted material which sells for more than its generic cousins. Caliper of grafted trees is measured two inches above the graft union. If age is given, it refers to the budded portion of the tree, with no concern for the age of the rootstock. When you buy grafted material, you are paying for someone else's expertise. How much that is worth to you depends on how much you can sell the material for when it is containerized. Before you make major investments in retail-ready bareroot, consider where you will be selling it. In many cases the bareroot grower has already claimed the major portion of the wholesale profits for growing it from seedling to retail-ready size and additional profit may only be found in retailing the product to the public or in growing the plants on to still larger sizes in larger containers.

FRUIT TREES

Fruit trees and flowering fruit trees are two areas of grafted bareroot where prices remain moderate and offer excellent profit potential in the short run. The production of deciduous fruit trees is only rarely done in containers. Almost all the commercial material is field grown and harvested bareroot. Deciduous fruit trees are the most common trees sold to the public in their bareroot state. Some retail nurseries still row out their trees in sawdust or sand beds, but now more people are familiar with the fruit trees packaged like roses, sold in the plastic bags with pictures of the mouth-watering fruit inviting you to buy the trees. Table 6.4 gives prices for unpackaged bareroot standard fruit trees.

Table 6.4 Standard fruit trees bareroot pricing

| peach   & | 5/16" | 3/8" | 1/2" | 5/8" | 3/4" | 1" |
nectarine						
	$3.80	$4.00	$4.20	$4.40	$4.50	$4.70
apricot	$4.40	$4.70	$5.10	$5.35	$5.45	$5.60
apple	$4.70	$5.10	$5.30	$5.80	$5.95	$6.05
cherry	$5.20	$5.70	$6.16	$6.45	$6.65	$6.90
plum	$3.80	$4.00	$4.20	$4.40	$4.50	$4.70

Dwarf trees are on different rootstocks and the prices run about $1.00 more for each grade.

Fruit trees are frequently graded by caliper alone. The price increase is very little extra for the increasing caliper. Height is of no importance with fruit trees since the tops are usually cut out in order to force lower branching, thereby keeping the fruit within easy picking range. Most nurseries like the 5/8" size tree because its roots fit well into the five gallon container without much pruning, and the size of the tree makes a good presentation to the customer. A 5/8" to 3/4" five gallon fruit tree wholesales between $9.00 and $11.00, and if planted in the biodegradable pulp pot, it is immediately marketable. However, keep in mind that the wholesale price for the newly container-ized tree is in many cases equivalent to a discount store's retail bareroot price.

Fruit trees are finished bareroot products which offer a good opportunity to turn your money quickly with little or no additional growing time. You can realize a higher selling price by going directly to the public, but you must know your market. If you are in an area of small yards, the homeowners may prefer the more expensive dwarf or semi-dwarf trees versus the standard size. Moreover, the prime marketing period for con-tainerized fruit trees begins after the bareroot season is over in

April and runs through June. A large number of fruit trees can be sold during this short period. After June the market slows to a crawl, and by fall retailers are discounting what they have left in order to make room for the next bareroot season.

A note here on citrus fruit trees: commercial production of citrus trees is limited to the warmer southern climates, due to the frost tender nature of the trees. Citrus is not sold bareroot since it is an evergreen. It used to be sold balled and burlapped, but it is most commonly grown and retailed today in containers. The grafted dwarfs are most popular with homeowners, while the standard trees remain the orchard trees. Occasionally, the trees are available from growers in deep liner pots which can be transplanted into fives. For anyone who intends to grow citrus, it is important to have some kind of frost protection available in case of severe winter conditions.

FLOWERING FRUIT TREES

The market is somewhat different for flowering ornamental fruit trees than for the fruiting varieties. The greatest demand for flowering crabapples, plums, cherries, and pears usually occurs during their blooming season, but the trees are frequently included in both residential and commercial landscaping plans, which keeps demand high all year round. Since flowering fruit trees are grafted onto the same types of rootstock as their fruiting cousins, some varieties are grown by the same growers who specialize in fruit trees. With these growers the prices tend to be only slightly higher than their fruiting trees. Always ask the grower whether the ornamental flowering fruit trees have been topped. This may not deter you from making the purchase since you may want to prune the trees once you containerize them, but at least with untopped trees you have the choice where to cut.

To find the greatest variety in flowering fruit trees, deal with growers who specialize in ornamental shade trees. There are hundreds of varieties of flowering fruit trees and not all are suited to every area, so market research is important. All large bareroot material is tied into bundles of five and ten, which allows you to buy in much smaller quantities than seedlings. You must still meet minimum order requirements, but instead of getting 50 or 100 of one variety you can order many different varieties in bundle quantities of five and ten and test market different items. Going through the catalogues and picking out different items is fun and we make it a point to buy something new every year and give it a try.

CHAPTER 7

STAGE FIVE: PRODUCTION IN CONTAINERS LARGER THAN FIVES

Five gallon containers mark the end of the move up line for most shrubs and vines, but plastic containers are also manufactured in seven, ten and fifteen gallon sizes. When conifers and shrubs are grown in larger containers, the sevens and fifteens are preferred. The tens and especially the fifteens are mostly used for trees. Pulp pots are also manufactured in larger sizes and are not commonly described by gallon volume but are catalogued by width and depth.

Table 7.1 Containers larger than #5s

type of pot	size #	capacity	# per case	@ price
black plastic	#7	1,403 cu.in.	20	$1.65
blow molded	#7	1,337 cu.in.	40	$1.17
pulp	15"x13"	1,732 cu.in.	16	$1.66
pulp	15"x16"	1,888 cu.in.	16	$1.82
black plastic	#10	1,922 cu.in.	10	$2.46
blow molded	#10	2,230 cu.in.	25	$2.30
pulp	18"x16"	2,411 cu.in.	12	$3.68
black plastic	#15	2,476 cu.in.	10	$2.70
blow molded	#15	2,494 cu.in.	25	$2.39
pulp	21"x12"	2,498 cu.in.	12	$4.56

Only the #15 plastic containers can readily be found used. In our area, landscapers sell used #15s for $1.00, which is a substantial savings over the prices of the new containers. But a dollar is a dollar, so it is important to inspect used #15s to make sure that they are not split or broken. When you have to throw a broken #15 away, it takes up a lot more room in your garbage than just throwing away the dollar you spent on it. Sometimes cracks and splits in the plastic are not easily seen until you have filled the container with soil and it bulges open at the split.

When inspecting the #15s, it is better to rely on your ear, rather than your eye, to detect defects. First, separate the containers from each other. This is not always easy since landscapers have a tendency to jam the cans together. If you have your 2" x 2" stick handy, you can knock them loose by hitting or prying against the rim. Once you have separated the cans, tap the bottom edge of each one on the ground, turning it as you tap. You will know what to listen for by simply comparing the sounds of a solid can with one that is split. Sorting by sound saves you time and is more accurate than just looking the cans over. If you do get containers which are damaged, you can salvage some by patching. Cut some plastic from a ruined container and cover the damaged spot with this extra piece of plastic. Soil will keep the patch in place.

As you increase the sizes of your containers, you also increase the weight factor and its demands on your back. A planted #7 weighs between fifty and sixty lbs. and a #15 between eighty-five and ninety-five lbs. A dolly is useful for moving your canned #15s into the growing area and saves you from lifting them into a wheelbarrow or onto a cart. With the #15s we have reached the last stage of material that can easily be handled by one person without lifting equipment. The weight may be the determining factor whether or not you want to handle plants in this size.

When you grow plants to larger sizes, the profit per unit increases dramatically. The cutting or seedling that you root and sell in a liner for $.60 can be grown through its stages and sold in a #15 for $25.00 or more. You make more money per unit, but spend more time growing each unit. In terms of maintenance, however, the #15 is the easiest of all to grow. Its higher selling price and longer holding period more than justify the initial overhead cost of a drip irrigation system. This frees you from the most time consuming aspect of maintenance. Without constant tending the time factor becomes less of a cost factor.

SHRUBS IN LARGE CONTAINERS

Most homeowners are content with their shrubs in ones or fives, preferring to let them grow rather than spend the extra money on larger plants. While the market for shrubs in #7s and #15s is small, there is still potential to be realized here since it is a market not heavily exploited. If it is your intention to market the larger sized containers to retail nurseries, it is best that you determine in advance the types of shrubs they are already stocking and discuss with the managers what other types of shrubs they would like to stock. Retailers are not willing to tie up large amounts of money in slow moving material. What the retail nurseries are willing to buy should be a guide to what you grow.

On the other hand, if you intend to sell directly to the public, the retail pricing of five gallon material may be your best sales aid in marketing larger size shrubs. When retail prices on five gallon shrubs approach $20.00, your larger plants in fifteens appear to the public to be bargains at $25.00, especially since a retailer is asking $50.00 to $85.00 for a #15.

If you transplant gallons into #7s and #15s, you must bypass the five gallon stage and wait the extra holding time needed for the plants to grow into the larger container size, just as was the case with liners into fives. You invest less in material and net a higher profit for waiting that extra growing time. Or as was the case with transplanting overgrown ones into fives, you can transplant overgrown #5s into #15s and substantially reduce growing time.

The #15 container is also very useful in rehabilitating shrubs which have gone astray. Sometimes plants become overgrown in the most unsightly ways, appearing woody, sparse and unbalanced. If you prune them and wait for them to grow back, you gain nothing extra for the waiting time and recovery may be slow. Transplant them into #15s where they can expand their root systems and reinvigorate themselves. Prune back the branches at the time of canning to promote new, fuller growth. While you are waiting for the plants to grow back, they are rooting in the larger containers and increasing in value.

BALLED AND BURLAPPED STOCK

A large percentage of nursery production is sold balled and burlapped, especially those plants that will not survive transplanting as bareroot. Larger conifers which were sold as bareroot seedlings and transplanted into fields where they have grown to bigger plants cannot be handled as bareroot, nor can larger field grown evergreen shrubs, such as rhododendrons. Instead of digging them from the ground and removing all the soil from their roots, the soil is kept in a ball around the roots and wrapped with burlap to keep it intact. Balled and burlapped plants are retail-ready products designed to be transplanted into the ground. The soil of their rootballs is usually heavy so that it will hold together in the shipping and handling. The burlap constitutes the container holding the soil around the rootball. B & B stock is sold during the dormant season, like bareroot, and cannot be held in the balled and burlapped state for long into the growing season when the plant needs regular watering. As the growing season progresses, unsold stock is containerized. Occasionally you can buy B & B material heavily discounted by retail stores which are not prepared to containerize the leftover stock.

B & B is finished product and offered for retail sale just as it is. No additional growing time is necessary. B & B is not a product for the backyard nurseryman to grow in containers, but one to resell as quickly as possible just as you resell retail-ready bareroot. Your customer is not likely to be the retailer who can buy the plants from the original grower for the whole-sale price, but there is good market potential in reselling directly to the public.

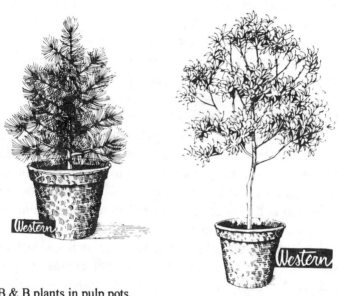

B & B plants in pulp pots.

If you have to containerize balled and burlapped stock, the large pulp containers are the best pots to use. The rootballs tend to be round and wide, and do not fit easily into the straight sided plastic containers. Fiber pots are wide at the top with a taper to the bottom which more naturally suits this material. Moreover, the pulp pots can be planted in the ground without further disturbing the rootball. When planting B & B material into containers, be careful not to handle the plant by the trunk and do not drop the plant, for you might break up the soil and tear away the roots. First, make sure your container is big enough to accommodate the rootball so that you do not have to jam it into the pot or have to extract it after you find it does not fit. You do not need a container much bigger than the width of the rootball. Put a small amount of soil in the bottom of the container. Position the plant so that its original ground line is about two inches below the rim. Do not remove the burlap from the soil; it will simply rot away and the roots will grow through it. Fill in the soil around the ball and tamp down. Cut the strings tying the burlap at the top of the ball and loosen the burlap at the soil line. Your plants are ready for immediate sale.

TREES

When it comes to trees, customers are much more willing to pay the higher price for a larger tree. They want shade in a hurry and are less interested in saving money than saving time. Moreover, larger trees have always been in heavy demand in commercial landscaping; consequently, the majority of material planted in #15s is trees. The marketable size of trees varies depending on variety, but generally trees in #15s are 1" or more in caliper and eight feet or more in height. This, of course, takes time to achieve, usually three years or more from seeds and cuttings. As with the shrubs, you can start by transplanting trees from one gallon containers. Although gallons cost more than bareroot seedlings, they can be bought in smaller quantities. Moreover, many of the varieties grown in containers are not even sold as bareroots. Many cultivars and grafted trees are produced only in containers. The grafting is done in liner pots or gallon containers and the plants are shifted up through the different stages. For example, Liquidambar Burgundy™ and Festival™ and Palo Alto™ are available in gallons at $5.75, but are not commonly offered for sale as small bareroots. Most wholesalers who grow one gallon trees are growing them to shift up into larger containers and occasionally they sell overstock to other growers; therefore, species grown and availability vary widely.

Five gallon trees, especially any overgrown trees, make excellent candidates for shifting into #15s and are much more frequently used than the smaller gallon trees. Not only does the overgrown five shorten the growing time to produce a #15, but it also eliminates the frustration that comes from having selected a one gallon tree which fails to grow in a proper manner. There is always a risk that the gallon tree not grow straight or that it not develop a good branching structure. If you do not correct problems at an early stage, they only grow worse and the tree becomes unsightly and unmarketable. Producing a beautiful specimen is much more likely when you select a well shaped five gallon tree to transplant into the #15.

Large bareroot trees heeled into soil awaiting transplanting.

BAREROOT GRAFTED AND CULTIVAR TREES

A large number of grafted trees are field grown and sold as retail-ready bareroot. The higher pricing of these trees makes them poor candidates for canning into five gallons if you intend to sell them on the wholesale market. But if you put them into #15s and grow them to a larger size, it is easy to more than double or triple your money in a six month period.

Some of the best trees to transplant into #15s are the bareroot flowering fruit trees which are very close in price to standard fruit trees. Although they cost less than other bareroot ornamental shade trees, the flowering fruit trees once planted into #15s can bring the same wholesale prices. For example, a purple leaf flowering plum of 1" caliper can be bought for $6.50, canned into a #15 for another $3.00, grown for three to four months and then sold for $25.00 to $30.00.

To determine what profit margins are possible with larger cultivar and grafted trees, consult catalogues for wholesale prices on #15s. The closer in price a bareroot gets to that wholesale price, the smaller your profit for containerizing it. Smaller, cheaper trees net a higher profit, but demand a longer growing time. The trick is to find the right size which will grow to a marketable #15 in the shortest time for the greatest profit. Tricks are learned from experience. Before you invest heavily in large, expensive bareroot, start with smaller, less expensive material and acquire some expertise in handling and growing bareroot.

Cultivar and grafted trees are not commonly available in small sizes as bareroots. They require more work, more time and more money from the grower. Most nurseries which specialize in cultivars do so with the intention of netting higher profits, a goal best realized by growing the plants to larger sizes, not selling the plants young. Moreover, the fact that the plants are grown in the ground prevents them from being sold except at the end of each growing season when they have reached larger sizes.

The grading of larger bareroot goes by 1/8" and 1/4" increments in caliper and by one to two foot increments in height. In its beginning stage, a deciduous tree rapidly grows a strong central leader and then begins to develop a branching head after it reaches some height. Trees which have not yet begun to develop lateral branches are called whips and are usually one year younger than the trees which have developed branching heads. Four to five foot whips are about the smallest size in which most bareroot cultivars and grafted ornamental trees are sold.

To get an idea how bareroot pricing of generic trees differs from their cultivar cousins and how prices of whips differ from branched trees, consider the catalogue pricing for red maples (acer rubrum) in Table 7.2.

Table 7.2 Red Maples

variety red maple	3-4' whip	4-5' whip	5-6' whip	6-8' branched
generic	$4.20	$5.45	$6.50	$9.80
Autumn Radiance	not sold	$7.30	$8.60	$15.20
October Glory	not sold	$8.50	$9.75	$18.75

Prices of the whips increase in small increments, but prices jump dramatically when the trees reach the 6-8' branched stage. The cultivars' branched prices are more than double that of their 4-5' whips, but the generic maple's price does not double for the same corresponding growth.

This pricing reveals that the grower makes more money for the year he spends growing the cultivar whip into a branched tree than for the time it takes him to produce the whip. But the first stage is the most costly in terms of production. It involves greater loss ratios suffered in starting the plant from tissue cuttings or grafting, and it also includes the price of the patent. On the other hand, the first year's growth of generic seedling maples is less costly than that of the cultivars, since the seedlings need no grafting or patent tags. Yet in the catalogue pricing of Table 7.2 the grower charges more for time spent growing the generic whip than the extra year for growing the branched tree. The pricing seems inverted, but it is perfect for a backyard nurseryman. It is easy to grow a nice red maple tree from seed or from inexpensive seedlings, but the patent laws and lack of grafting expertise can prevent you from propagating cultivars.

However, since a grower of cultivar varieties makes more on the later years of growth than the first, it is easier and more profitable to enter into the production line at a later stage and grow the tree from a whip into a branched tree.

Growing cultivar whips into branched trees in #15s gives you flexibility the bareroot grower does not have. You have the ability to market the containerized plants as soon as they develop branched heads; the bareroot grower has to wait to dig his crop from the field at the end of the growing season. This allows you to have material available when the primary producer cannot service the market.

MANAGING YOUR INVESTMENT
AND YOUR TIME

Now that you understand how container growing is divided into stages, you can better determine ways to manage your investment. Never forget that plants in containers are not money in the bank and any living product is perishable. The longer you hold a plant, the greater the possibility something can go wrong. After investing capital in plants, it is always a comfort to see its safe return as quickly as possible.

There are many ways to minimize your investment risks and maximize your profits. Consider these three different strategies for fifteen gallon containers. Canning costs for these examples are based on used containers, soil costing $20.00 per yard and time release fertilizer added to the soil. No consideration is given for loss or different rates of growth which are variables.

EXAMPLE 1: Buy large bareroot seedlings, plant half into #5s and half into #15s

Buy 100 4-5' bareroot seedlings at $1.35 per tree. Can fifty into #5s at a cost of $.95 each for the canning. Your per tree cost is $2.30 which is an investment of $115 for these fifty #5 trees. If you put the other fifty into #15s at a cost of $3.00 each for canning, you have $4.35 invested per #15, for a total of $217.50 for these fifty. This brings your total investment to

$332.50. Your five gallon trees are marketable within six months. At a value of $9.00 each, you need to sell only thirty-seven trees to recover the full amount you have invested. The other thirteen five gallon trees are profit and every fifteen gallon tree is already paid for, canning and all. You can afford to wait for the fifteens to grow to a value of $25.00 each. They represent a profit potential of $1250.00 with no capital at risk.

EXAMPLE 2: Sell some of the bareroot seedlings immediately and can the remainder into #15s.

Buy the 4-5' seedlings for $1.35 each. You have purchased a plant which the retail-ready bareroot grower is wholesaling for $5.80. Immediately resell some of these trees in their bareroot state at prices competitive with the other wholesaler. If you sell at $3.00, your price represents a $1.65 profit per tree to you, and to your customer it represents a $2.80 savings over the $5.80 price charged by the other grower. Every tree you sell at $3.00 returns your investment on the one you sold and pays for one you containerize. If you sell fifty trees at $3.00 each, the fifty you put in containers are free. If you market the bareroot at $4.00 instead of $3.00, you begin to pay for canning costs as well. This strategy also works well with the larger retail-ready bareroot and with one and five gallon plants, if you can retail them directly to the public.

EXAMPLE 3: Purchase small seedlings and can all into #5s, sell some and transfer others later into #15s.

Purchase 100 2-3' seedlings at a cost of $70.00. Can all 100 into #5s at a cost of $95.00 for canning. Total investment is $165. When the trees become marketable at $9.00, you need to sell only nineteen to recover your full investment. This leaves eighty-one #5s worth $729.00. Continue selling throughout the season and transfer only what did not sell into #15s. If you sell another sixty-one trees for $549.00 and transplant the last twenty into #15s, subtracting from your profits the canning cost of $2.70 each (you need less soil for the #15 when you transplant a #5), your net profit is $495.00 and you still have $500.00 worth of trees in #15s at no cost. Your original investment at no time exceeds $165.00 and your profit potential is almost $1000.00.

It is fun to devise your own strategies. The variations are endless. When you can grow trees in your own backyard with no capital investment at risk, then money really does grow on trees.

Plants continue to sell in container sizes beyond #15s, moving up into #20 plastic cans and then into 24", 36" and 48" wooden boxes. The same principles continue to apply as already discussed, but a #15 is really about the most weight a man can easily lift onto a truck by himself, so we end our treatment of container growing stages here and turn now to the topic of how to produce a quality plant.

CHAPTER 8

HOW TO PRODUCE A QUALITY PLANT

DETERMINING STANDARDS OF QUALITY

In order to know what the marketplace considers a quality plant, you need some kind of standard to give you an idea what the plant should look like in size and overall appearance. Make the rounds of the local retail nurseries and inspect their stock, especially the varieties you are growing. The fact that particular plants are in the beds offered for sale indicates that the retailer feels that they are marketable. Plants cannot be manufactured to predetermined industry standards, so you will find that quality varies from one nursery to another. If a nursery tends to cater to the high end customer, the plants are usually purchased from growers with an established reputation for dependably high quality. These plants are usually larger and fuller and have a slightly higher wholesale cost. On the other hand, the discount stores, while not unconcerned with quality, want a market edge which depends on price. They may buy from wholesalers whose plants are younger, hence smaller in size and cheaper in price. The customer they are targeting prefers to pay less on the assumption that the plant will grow.

Although catalogue pricing is by the size of the container, not the size of the plant, every wholesale nursery sets a price based on its own minimum standard which the plant must reach before it is considered marketable. The ingredient that any nursery is adding to the plant is time, and time is what is adding to the size of the plant. With less time invested the plant is smaller, and with less time invested the plant is cheaper. A retailer expects to receive smaller plants for the smaller price from a grower using a lower standard of quality. Isn't this saying that the size of the plant determines the price of the plant? Yes and no. Yes, in that the grower has determined a price for his minimum standard; no, in that, if his plants should far exceed his minimum standard, reaching into that range of being overgrown, they still sell for no more than the catalogue listed price for that container size.

Market conditions also have a big influence on what is an acceptable size. When there is a shortage of a certain variety, its unavailability in larger sizes makes the retailers willing to accept plants of lower quality which would normally be rejected. Even the grower may feel that the size is too small for normal quality, but if the retailer is willing to accept it in that size, the grower will sell it. Likewise, if there is a glut on the market, plants continue growing while waiting to be sold and eventually become overgrown and younger plants, which were once perfectly acceptable, are rejected as too small compared to what else is available. Seeing what the retail nurseries are offering for sale is market research that you should do every time you visit the store.

PRUNING AND STAKING

Let's look at what is common to almost all plants and what appearance makes them most marketable and most profitable. If you are using time release fertilizer every time you containerize a plant, you have taken the first and most important step: you have assured the plant a constant and adequate supply of nutrients for even and extended growth. This is especially true for bedding plants and herbaceous perennials which need little in the way of shaping.

Trees, shrubs and vines need more tending and it is important to understand how these plants put on new growth, not the detailed chemical explanation, just the simple fact that they grow from the top up, not from the ground up. Unlike hair and grass which grow from the roots, trees, shrubs and vines grow from the ends of their branches or stems. A tree which has side branches starting three feet above the ground will always have those branches three feet from the ground; the trunk does not grow any higher out of the ground.

Sometimes a plant grows along quite happily, not caring if its right side is two feet longer than its left, or if its trunk is growing like a slithering snake. There are people who like this look and the bonsai market in particular searches for the odd shape, but many more people tend to like balance and straightness. To produce this, corrections are sometimes in order. Corrections are made in two ways: pruning and staking. Pruning involves cutting off some of that growth you have been so anxious to produce. As you stand there looking at the plant, trying to decide where to cut, you get the feeling that it is going to hurt you more than it hurts the plant. Pruning is shaping and there are basically only two ways to go. Cut off the tips of the plant, the plant will bush out; cut off the side branches, the plant will grow taller on the central trunk. Let's see how this applies to the three main types of larger plants: shrubs, trees and vines.

SHRUBS

A shrub is distinguished from a tree by having several low branching stems rather than a central trunk. Another name for a shrub is a bush and the adjective "bushy" is used to describe the leafy fullness of shrubs. There is virtually no pruning done on the young plants as they grow in the liner stage. However, when the liner is canned into a gallon container, it is common to pinch off the top of the plant in order to force the lower branching that makes the plant a bushy shrub. As the plant continues to grow, additional pruning may be done on the tips of the branches. Along the stems, wherever the plant has leaves or has had leaves, there are buds or nodes from which new branches can develop. By cutting just above these leaf nodes you force the plant to put the nutrients into those remaining buds. Usually a number of buds sprout along the stem creating denser growth. When you trim back the tip growth evenly around a whole shrub you reduce the width, eventually producing a tighter, fuller plant.

In the short run, pruning often significantly reduces the attractiveness of the plant, not only reducing the plant in size, but also exposing branches bare of leaves. It is very difficult to market such a plant until it has grown out into a fuller shape. Therefore, it is best to prune your plants each time they are transplanted. You have already committed yourself to waiting for the roots to fill out the larger container and the plant can spend that same time filling out the top growth as well. By the time the plant has developed a good root system, it should also have developed fairly balanced and full top growth.

Plants need to get even light on all sides in order to promote full and balanced growth. If you place your plants in their growing area can-to-can with no spacing between, eventually they become crowded and do not grow evenly. If you have room to spread them out, do so when you move them into their growing area; if not, or if you are trying to maximize space, sell the largest plants early in order to make room for the remainder. A plant reaching for light gets what is called leggy when its branches stretch out leaving little growth along the stem and a lonely bunch of leaves on the tips. Normally you will have to cut the plant back severely to promote fuller growth.

Sometimes you can use unsightly legginess to create something special. A number of shrubs can be trained into tree forms and this utilizes the other pruning option. If you have allowed a shrub to get away from you by growing long sparse branches, see if there is a strong central branch called a leader. To make the shrub into a tree form, cut away all the other branches except that central leader. Trim off some of the side growth along its trunk leaving only a few small shoots. Do not cut the top of the leader. This type of pruning promotes height in the single central leader and also encourages thicker caliper in the trunk. Stake the leader in order to support it and to keep it growing straight. Once it has reached the height where you want it to begin branching, cut out the top. This puts the growth into the lateral buds and the head of a tree begins to form.

These azaleas each developed a single tall leader. The rest of the plant is cut off at the base and the leader staked to produce a tree.

Training shrubs into trees is an area of specialty production which may be a profitable niche market for you. A photinia which sells for $6.50 in bush form can sell for $10.00 or more in tree form, yet it is the same plant in either form. Shrubs which can be trained into trees are listed in Table 8.1.

Table 8.1 Shrubs which can be trained into trees

abutilon	euryops	laurus
azalea	fuchsia	ligustrum
callistemon	gardenia	nerium
camellia	hibiscus	photinia
cercis	ilex	punica
cotinus	juniperus	pyracantha
escallonia	lagerstroemia	raphiolepis
eugenia	lantana	

TREES

Since a strong central leader is the main feature which distinguishes a tree from a shrub, the most important aspect of tree production becomes the creation of a straight trunk. When looking at the two foot diameter trunks of stately old trees, there is no sign of what might have once been a crooked trunk, but when a tree is young every little bend or twist stands out. A tree which is too crooked is difficult to sell and unacceptable in the retail nursery. Many of these trees are sold only at reduced prices as conservation grade material which is used in wild, natural settings. Many more are not sold at all, but simply discarded as culls.

Since a straight trunk translates into greater marketability and profit, staking is commonly used in nursery tree production despite the current recommendations by arborists that trees be grown unstaked, untrimmed and untopped. The natural sway of a tree in breezes and the diversion of growth into the lower branches contribute to a strengthening of the trunk. Staking and trimming away the lower growth produces an artificially forced tree which cannot support itself without the stake which is unnatural. And yet crooked is natural but unsightly, so what do you do?

It is more expensive to stake than not to stake, so begin by not staking. Give the tree a chance to grow straight on its own. You can do a couple things to promote this. By placing the trees can-to-can at the beginning of their growing cycle, you re-create the appearance of a small forest. The competition for light encourages their natural tendency to grow straight up. Moreover, the closeness of the trees offers some support and protection in winds that can easily bend over a lone tree. When you get the trees to a reasonable height, spread them apart in order to encourage top branching. The newer theory on growing shade trees is never to cut the central leader, but sometimes it just heads for the sun and produces no branches unless topped. You will have to use your own judgment on topping, but we have found it necessary on some trees and the results have been good.

Remember that the lower side growth promotes thicker caliper in the truck. Do not cut all the lower branches off the tree while it is young. If you leave trees too close together for a long time, the lower branches will begin to die off when they get no light. This is a natural process for most trees, but not something you want on screening trees, such as liquidambars. Space these types of trees further apart when you notice branches beginning to die back. There comes a time when you have to straighten out the trees which did not get with the program. The newer theory on staking is to put the stake several inches to the side of the plant and not tie it tightly to the stake. While this helps straighten a bending trunk, it does nothing to correct an already crooked one. To straighten out a badly shaped tree, it must be tied to the stake. Drive the stake in close to the trunk. Starting at the bottom of the tree, tie it tightly to the stake with plastic tree tie. Work your way up the trunk pulling it to the stake, tying as you go. If the tree is very top heavy or too tall to reach the top, lay it down on the ground to tie it. You will be surprised what you can straighten out this way.

At other times you may have allowed a plant to grow in a completely unacceptable way. Say you have a tree, or a shrub which can be made into a tree, growing on over the edge of the can to one side and almost running on the ground, you can still make quite a nice tree. In a case like this, do not try to bend the leader all the way up, it will break. Simply transplant it into a larger container, turning the rootball of the plant so the central leader is about as upright as you can get it and then stake it. The rootball may look odd tilted like that, but just plant it deep enough so that the soil covers it completely. The roots do not care and what appeared worthless becomes a valuable tree.

Generally, a 5' to 6' tall by 1" wide stake is used on five gallon trees and a 6' to 8' by 2" stake is used on larger trees in fifteens. Since the stake is constantly exposed to water you need something that does not rot quickly. Rough redwood or treated fir are most common and can be purchased from nursery supply houses. The local lumber yard is another source and is usually less expensive. If the lumber yard does not carry stakes, ask if they are willing to strip some larger boards into stakes for you. Points on the end may cost extra, but this is not really necessary in order to pound them into the loose soil of the nursery containers. An excellent, inexpensive alternative to wood stakes is bamboo. In fact, bamboo is even sturdier than wood. The 1/2" bamboo stake is equivalent to the strength of the 1" wood stake. Some prices for stakes from a nursery supply company are given in Table 8.2.

There is also a recycle market for used stakes. Landscapers usually restake a tree when they plant it, simply discarding the old stake. There is still utility in that stake, but you have to be careful. The portion which has been in wet soil for a long time is prone to breaking. If you need to use the stake a long time, avoid the used stake; but if you are simply straightening something prior to sale, a used stake works just fine. You can also cut off the portion of the stake that has been in the dirt and has deteriorated.

Table 8.2   Stakes

type	size	# per bundle	@ price
redwood	1/2"x1/2"x36"	25	$.20
redwood	1/2"x1/2"x48"	25	$.24
redwood	1"x1"x4'	25	$.44
redwood	1"x1"x5'	25	$.54
redwood	1"x1"x6'	25	$.56
bamboo	3/8"x4'	1,000	$.08
bamboo	1/2"x6'	250	$.25
bamboo	3/4"x6'	200	$.48
bamboo	1/2"x7'	250	$.30
bamboo	1"x8'	100	$.85
treated fir	2"x2"x8'	10	$3.00

VINES

By nature, a vine needs something to climb on, otherwise it is just a spreading ground cover. Right from the beginning, vines in gallon containers should be staked with 3' to 4' by 1/2" stakes. It is also a good idea to give your vines some separation from other plants or they will entwine themselves among their neighbors. When you transplant vines into five gallon cans, restake with 6' by 1" wooden stakes. Wrap the vine loosely around the stake, tying as you go. Vines in five or fifteen gallon cans can also be tied up on trellises. Trellised vines are specialty items which sell for much higher prices. The trellis, however, can cost more than the plant and the canning combined, unless you make your own.

Making your own trellis is easy. Purchase the wood and staples from a lumberyard. You can hammer the staples or use a good staple gun that can penetrate the thickness of the wood. To make a pattern for your trellis, break down a cardboard box for a large flat piece of cardboard. Trace around a trellis you have bought, or design your own and draw out the lines on the cardboard. With the pattern drawn out, all you have to do is lay out the pieces within the lines and fasten them together. After making sure your trellis is solid, pound it into the soil of the planted container. Wrap the vine around the wood and tie it so it stays put. Once started, most vines continue wrapping themselves around the trellis as they grow.

PESTICIDES

Your plants should be free of insects and disease at the time of delivery. From time to time you have to deal with these problems. Most pest control in wholesale nurseries is achieved by spraying either insecticides which kill insects, or by spraying fungicides which kill fungus. When used separately an insecticide will not kill fungus, nor will a fungicide kill an insect. Many garden sprays labeled as All Purpose contain both an insecticide and a fungicide. The pesticides on the garden shop shelves are labeled for home use and considered safe if used according to directions. It is most unlikely that you will ever need anything stronger. The government regulations regarding the use of pesticides are becoming ever more stringent and it is a good idea to check with your county department of agriculture as to what restrictions apply. Moreover, you do not want to get on the wrong side of your neighbors by using chemicals that bother them. But most of all, remember that you are the one living and working in the area where you use the pesticides, so common sense and following regulations are to your benefit.

Some nursery operations have a program of preventive spraying, others do spraying only when there is a visible problem. Preventive spraying of fungicide is very effective in controlling fungus disease and quite necessary on many plants especially in the winter and early spring. However, preventive spraying for insects can have a very deleterious effect. Just as every plant seems to have something which eats it, so too every insect has a natural predator which eats it. But an insecticide cannot distinguish between beneficial and harmful insects; it will kill the good with the bad. Preventive spraying of insecticide means constant spraying, because the insecticide eliminates the good insects with the bad, leaving only the spray as a means of control on the harmful population. We use insecticides when necessary, but we prefer to avoid them if possible. We are always willing to give the predator insects a chance to eat the harmful insects. Just how effective natural controls can be was proven by California's Department of Agriculture. In order to control a white fly infestation, it imported and bred a tiny wasp, smaller than a period on this page. The wasp quickly overcame a white fly population which had proven impossible to eradicate with pesticides.

Giving the natural predators time to do their job may leave your plant unsalable for a slightly longer time than if insecticides were used, but since you are living in the same environment as your plants, you have to decide how often you want to use insecticides. The use of any pesticides at all has become a real health issue and led to a major movement for the production of organic vegetables. Ornamental plant material is not eaten, but residue from spray still exists on the plants and on the ground. Some of these environmental problems are addressed with the development and use of insecticidal soaps rather than more toxic chemicals.

Keep in mind that a healthy plant, like a healthy body has natural resistance to most diseases and insects. Fertilizer and proper watering are the two most important elements you can provide toward maintaining a healthy plant. When an outside threat does appear, you have to decide whether the threat is minor, and one that the plant and the natural environment can handle on its own, or if it is critical, requiring your intervention. Certain plants have more problems with fungus, others with insects, others are virtually trouble free. This chapter does not deal with the specific problems of insects and disease which affect different species in different ways. Other books can advise you better on the specifics of what to do for what you are growing. Your local agricultural advisors and university agricultural extension services can also provide help and information on the problems that are bugging you.

CHAPTER 9

HOW DO YOU MARKET YOUR PRODUCT?

SELLING TO THE RETAILER:
PRELIMINARY CONSIDERATIONS

Before you offer your plants for sale to any nursery, assess your competition. First, determine if the plants you intend to sell are of sufficient quality to offer to a retail nursery. By visiting retail stores, you can determine how your plants compare in quality with those the retailer already has in stock. If yours are comparable, then you have a product which will not face rejection as substandard and you can approach your customer with a fair degree of confidence in your product. The second thing you need to know is what price to ask for your product. Your production cost has very little bearing on what your plant is worth, since the larger wholesale market determines the price. In your initial process of gathering information, you collected catalogues from wholesale nurseries and studied their plant lists and pricing. You found that not all pricing is the same. In part this reflects certain standards which each nursery has set for the quality of its plants as discussed in the last chapter. Comparison of catalogue listings gives you both the bottom and the top prices of the wholesale market. Unless you have a plant which no one else is growing, it is reasonable to assume that these prices will set the range within which you can price your plants.

There is one factor which can increase the catalogue's list price of the plant. The wholesaler often adds a shipping charge. Most catalogue pricing is FOB point of origin, which means that the plants are loaded onto the truck free, but transportation is extra. The shipping charge is usually calculated on a per can basis depending on the size of the containers and the zone into which the plants are shipped. Sometimes a flat rate is charged; sometimes on large orders the shipping charge is waived. Shipping is a real cost factor and must be added to the list price when charged. In most cases, your own local deliveries can be made without shipping costs and this can give you an edge.

The printed catalogue price, however, does not tell all and there are other things to consider before you set your price. Many wholesalers offer discounts which reduce the list price. Discounts are given on large quantity purchases either on multiples of a single variety or on the dollar volume of the whole order. There are discounts on prepayment of orders, or on cash payment on delivery or payment within 10 days. All such discounts are specified in the grower's catalogue, and you can offer the same kinds of discounts. But there are also discounts not mentioned. Sometimes these discounts are given to members of trade associations and may be as large as 20% off the list price. Sometimes discounts are negotiated between the parties. And, of course, a grower may decide to put an item on sale in order to reduce inventory or to bring his prices in line with current market conditions. If you are using other growers' catalogues to help set your prices, you need to take discounts into consideration before you set your prices. If you have determined on too high a price for your product, the retailer may simply say that he can get the plants from other suppliers for less. The option is yours to meet or beat the other prices he quotes, but it also helps to know if those quoted prices are real or just bargaining chips.

There are also factors other than price which influence a retailer's purchasing decisions. Most larger wholesalers extend credit to retailers. It is fairly standard in the industry to give the retailers thirty days to pay their bills, allowing them time to sell some or all of the material before the bill comes due. This is leverage which allows them to work on other people's money. Offering credit is a common sales tool used by wholesalers. The most extreme example is the special future order offered in the fall or winter in order to secure a major portion of spring business. The retailer can reserve material for delivery in the spring and receive a greatly extended credit period. Billing is deferred for months. Not only do retailers get the inventory without having to make immediate payment, but they get to use the money generated from the sales interest free for several months.

Wholesalers are not doing this out of the goodness of their hearts. At the start of the selling season, cash is tight in the retail nursery which has just gone through winter, its slowest season of the year. The offer to defer payment is a most attractive inducement to the retailer who has not yet seen the cash flow improve with spring sales. The object of the future order is for a wholesaler to get as many of his plants into the store as possible for that rush of spring business. The more plants he stocks, the less opportunity for the competition. Even an attractive price by another supplier may not be enough to get the cash-poor retailers to buy less expensive items which must be paid for sooner. Moreover, when retailers lock themselves into commitments months ahead of time for plants to be delivered in the spring, they are not interested in buying from another grower until they have taken delivery and sold their future order. In other words, even though you see holes which you think you can fill in spring, an undelivered future order may temporarily freeze you out of the market. The future order is only a one time a year offer, so when the material is sold the doors are open again.

You have to decide if you are willing to extend credit to a retailer. Some retailers are more inclined to simply pay a small grower for small orders upon delivery. This is best for you. If they offer to pay on delivery, take it. But others may ask if you will give them thirty days, which is the standard in the industry. In a business selling time, offering credit is just part of selling more time, and we always figure that it is better that someone else is watering and taking care of the plants for those thirty days, so we are willing to wait. If a retailer fails to pay as agreed at the end of thirty days, usual contract terms impose a 1 1/2% interest charge per month on late payments. In practice this is seldom collected by the wholesaler who is happy just to have the slow pay customer settle his account. If you do business with slow pay customers, you need to re-assess your continuing business relationships with those customers.

GUARANTEE OR NON-GUARANTEE

What kind of a guarantee does the retailer expect from you? Most growers' catalogues contain terms and conditions of sale regarding guarantees and limitations on liability. Wholesale material is sold "as is" with no warranty, expressed or implied, as to quality, description, marketability, productivity, viability or anything else. Upon delivery it is the responsibility of the retailer to inspect the material to make sure that it is healthy, pest free and true to name. Claims on unsatisfactory material must be made in writing usually within five to seven days. The liability clause in the conditions of sale limits any claim for damage to the price of the unsatisfactory material.

Basically then, you make every effort to deliver quality, true to name, pest free nursery stock, but you do not warrant anything. However, if any problem is brought to your attention by your customers, work with them on a solution. If the problem can be shown to have originated with you, it is good business to make the adjustment. Even if you know that something was not your fault, you might want to fix it just to keep goodwill.

INVOICING

Invoicing your customer does not require an elaborate computer set-up, although if you have a computer you can certainly use it for billing. A standard duplicating or triplicating receipt book is really all that is necessary. When you deliver plants to any business customer, have an invoice drawn up listing the plants by variety, size, quantity and price. Make sure that an employee is there to receive and inspect the material as it is unloaded. Confirm the count and that the plants are in good condition, and have the employee sign the invoice. This is the only way you can prove that the plants were delivered and were accepted in good condition by your customer. Usually you leave a copy of the delivery invoice with the customer and it serves as the billing invoice. If a company wants a separate billing invoice mailed to their office, make sure that you have written the order in triplicate so that you can leave a copy at the time of delivery and send one for billing and keep a copy for your records.

MAKING THE SALE

A basic understanding of what the competition customarily offers the retailer in plant quality, pricing and terms helps you better assess where you, the small grower, can fit in as a supplier to retail nurseries. There are basically two kinds of retailers in the nursery trade: the chain store owned by a large, regional or national corporation, and the locally owned and operated nursery which may have one or more locations.

THE LOCALLY OWNED NURSERY

The simplest places to start with are the locally owned nurseries, especially with the stores where you have already been doing business buying your gardening supplies. If you have already established a relationship with the owner as his customer, he will be quite willing to take a look at what you have grown.

The other retailers in your area can be found by consulting the yellow pages of the phone book under the listing of Nurseries, Retail. When you make your initial contact, do not simply phone and ask if they want to buy some plants. Of course they want to buy some plants, but they have no idea who you are or what the plants look like. Your initial contact should be made in person. Use the phone book to get the addresses, and start with the nurseries closest to your home.

If you just walk in with a list of what you have available and hand it to someone, it will almost certainly get lost. So how do you make that first sale? In the beginning it may seem difficult to compete against established suppliers, but there are a number of things that occur naturally in the business that create windows of opportunity for the small grower. No matter how attractive and professional a catalogue from a large grower may look, no matter how many varieties of plants it may list, it cannot guarantee that the nursery always has them ready for sale. It frequently happens that a grower sells out of one crop of plants and will not have another crop ready for sale for many weeks or even months. If you have the plants ready and the retailer's regular supplier is out of them, you have found a window. And again, no matter how many trucks a company has, it will not always have enough orders to fill a trailer and may not be able to deliver for a couple of weeks until it can get a sufficient load. If the retailer needs the plants right away, you have found another window. A retailer may run out of only a couple varieties of plants; he needs them, but does not want to make up an order to meet the minimum required by the large wholesaler. If you are willing to deliver with no set minimum sale requirement, you have another window.

Keep in mind, however, that a retailer is not going to buy plants he does not need. Before you even try to talk to someone about buying your plants, tour the nursery looking for the types of plants you have ready for sale. If the beds are well stocked with your varieties, it is not likely the retailer will order more until he has sold some of the existing stock. You can enhance your chances of finding empty beds needing re-stocking if you visit the nursery on a Monday. The weekend is the busiest time of the week for retail nurseries and Monday or Tuesday is when they inventory to determine what to reorder. By Thursday or Friday the beds should be restocked and ready for the weekend. If you find your varieties of plants well stocked, you are inviting rejection by trying to sell something for which there is no immediate or apparent need. You can by-pass rejection by going directly to the next nursery on your list and checking its stock. When you find a bed that is low or empty, or one in which the remaining material is substandard, you have identified where there is a need and you are there to fill it.

Now is the time to approach your potential buyer. With any established business you will have to assume that someone has been supplying them with product and that certain comfortable business relationships exist. You are an unknown and the buyer has no idea what your plants look like. Therefore, be prepared to show what you have. When you are making your first calls on nurseries, take along some plants as samples to show what your material looks like. Do not take the very best, if there are only a couple of examples like it, but take plants representative of the majority of what you have available. If the buyer likes what you offer, the next question will be what the plants cost. Having researched catalogue list prices, you should have a price in mind that sounds reasonable and attractive. This is the point at which you are expecting to get the order: you have the plants which are needed and you just quoted one of the best prices in the marketplace. And sometimes it works just like it is supposed to, but there is always a way that your fish can throw your hook. Your customer can stall, saying that he has to check the orders he has already placed to make sure that he has not ordered the plants from his usual supplier. It is difficult to get someone to leave the comfort zone of doing business with familiar faces. In this case, offer to check back later to find out if he has ordered the plants or if he does indeed need them. Once you have promised to call back, be sure that you do. It never hurts to check back on Friday to see if the empty bed has been refilled for the weekend. It frequently happens that although the order was placed with another nursery, the plants are not shipped or are rejected upon delivery.

In other selling situations you may have to get down to brass tacks. Yes, we are talking price. Pricing your plants below normal wholesale is a strong inducement for the retailer to buy your product. It is the retailer's choice whether to pass along the savings to the customer and increase profit through volume or simply increase profit by holding to the regular price. In either case, high quality plants at lower prices are always attractive to the retailer.

Making that first sale opens the door, but it does not a relationship make. That is something that can only develop over time. Do not expect a retailer to call you when he sells your plants. The regular salesman will be there the following Monday looking to fill the holes. You have to continue to visit the nurseries and check the beds. Once the retailer has gotten to know you and your quality, you will be able to check back by phone, but it will never be a substitute for making that personal appearance and checking on what else you can market. It is only by having good quality, adequate quantity, competitive pricing and marketing persistence that you can earn a position as a regular supplier.

On the other hand, becoming a regular weekly supplier may not be your goal. Your preference may be to grow and sell one or two seasonal crops. For example, your goal may be to produce 2,000 gallons of perennial color which you start growing in March with the intention of selling out by October so that you can use the money for a winter vacation. Neither your crop nor your customers need you the rest of the year. Work to establish a reputation for producing a quality plant at a good price so that whenever your crop is ready for market, the retailer can depend on you and is looking forward to an adequate supply. A retailer may find it advantageous to use your whole crop as an ad item for seasonal promotions. Such a niche will give you a dependable market year after year, yet will not tie you to your business year-round.

CONSIGNMENT SELLING

One thing to keep in mind when it comes to marketing your crop is that you own it and you can be flexible in your marketing approach. You can negotiate price, set terms and deliver on short notice. In some cases you may even decide to sell on consignment. This means that you deliver the material to the retailer who has no commitment to purchase your product at all, but offers it for sale in his store, only paying you for what sells. In these cases you may be able to get a slightly higher price for your plants because the retailer has nothing at risk. If the plants do not sell, they are returned to you without payment. Consignment selling may be the way for you to get your foot in the door and to initially do business with a nursery, but ultimately it requires greater effort to keep track of your inventory, and to motivate a retailer to sell material that does not sell itself.

THE RETAIL CHAIN STORE

The large corporations have a different way of doing business than the small locally owned companies. The chain store's home office exercises a certain amount of control over the purchases made on the local level. For example, most department managers cannot order merchandise from vendors who are not on the company's list of approved vendors. To get on the list, each vendor must undergo a corporate approval process and enter into a contract which sets forth the terms on which business will be done. You must provide a price list and your terms of sale. Chain stores want more time for payment and usually you have to give them sixty days. Moreover, these stores are on computer systems using bar code pricing so they require the more expensive bar code labeling. Demands may also be made that you deliver to a certain number of stores in the area and monetary penalties may be levied against you if deliveries are not made on time.

The contract terms which may put the damper on the smaller grower are the indemnification clause and the requirement that you carry an insurance policy for $1,000,000 for vendor and product liability. This protects the corporation from any possible lawsuit resulting from injuries sustained by your product. Even though plants seem harmless, compared to power equipment, liability insurance is required of all of their vendors. This kind of insurance is usually carried by the large growers, but is an overhead expense seldom assumed by smaller growers. Product liability insurance may be hard to find and expensive in the open market, but it is available to members of nurserymen associations at better rates. The chain stores also require that you carry a $1,000,000 policy on your vehicle, which is usually available through your regular carrier.

These terms are fairly standard for chain stores. Personally contact the nursery manager in one of the stores to find out how a particular chain does business. If the manager does not have the authority to buy on the local level, except from the approved list of vendors, get the name and phone number of the person you must talk to in the home office. If you can produce a sufficient volume of material to stock several stores and if you are in a position to meet their terms and standards, you may find that the chain store generates such a volume of business that it is the only account you need.

GROCERY AND DRUG STORES

More and more grocery stores and drug stores carry nursery stock. House plants and floral plants are sold inside the store. Bedding plants and vegetable starts, flowering perennials and roses are the favored items sold outside. The emphasis is on flowering plants since they are impulse items. General landscape shrubs and trees are less frequently offered. The distinction between chain stores and locally owned stores discussed above still applies. Contact the manager of the drug store and the produce manager at the grocery store in order to find out how they do business.

WHOLESALE NURSERIES

As we said in the beginning chapter, most gardeners have had little or no experience with the wholesale nursery which grows plants for the retail and landscape trade. The preceding chapters on the various stages of production have dealt with how to purchase from wholesalers, but you should not think of these growers only as a source of material or as potential competition in the marketplace. Not all growers start their own material, and growers are always buying from other growers. There is a great deal of potential in selling to the wholesale market. However, as we have seen, a grower is interested in getting plants ready for the peak retail season which demands a certain amount of lead time for production. This means that a grower wants the transplant material at earlier times in the production cycle than the retailer. These planting times will vary depending on what is being grown. If you intend to find a niche in marketing to other growers, you will have to talk with them in advance about their various needs for material and the timing.

One of the most common types of purchases made by growers is the liner stock which is transplanted into #1s. Since the wholesale growers need to have their crops planted in time to sell at the peak marketing season, they must have a dependable supply of material available when they need it. Contracting for the plants is one of the chief ways to assure availability. Much of the liner business is done strictly on contract basis. The customer determines when he will need the material and adequate lead time must be given in order to grow the plants. Time varies with the species to be grown, so a supplier must have sufficient experience in growing the contracted plants in order to have them ready on time. For a person just starting in business, contracting is not likely to be your first transaction, since neither you nor your customer can be sure you will fulfill the contract. Initially you may begin by speculating on the market demands, showing that you can produce the plants at the right time. As your experience increases, so too will your confidence in your ability to meet market timetables.

Contracting is a form of business which can provide you with a comfortable and dependable market. The terms of any contract can be negotiated between the parties, but the basics that are important to the buyer are: 1) a statement of minimum standards for the plants, 2) the delivery date, 3) a stated quantity and 4) the price. The seller is interested in all of the above terms, but also wants some kind of reasonable assurance that the buyer will perform. A deposit is generally required, usually in the range of 25% to 33%. Should the buyer fail to perform, it then becomes the buyer's responsibility to find another buyer or forfeit the deposit. Should the seller fail to perform, a disclaimer clause is usually included for failure to perform due to reasons beyond the grower's control.

The advantages to the buyer are that he usually negotiates a better price and has a fair degree of assurance that he will have the plants when needed. The advantages to the seller are that he knows exactly what to grow, how many, when to have them ready and for whom. These advantages are worth the concessions made in the price.

Besides needing plants for shifting up to larger containers, there are also occasions when wholesalers buy plants from other growers for resale to their customers. Once we were given an opportunity to bid some plants on a large landscape plan. The landscaper showed us the prices already bid by a large company. For the most part, the prices were quite low, even below what we were willing to sell the material for. However, a few fairly common items were bid at higher prices out of line with the other plants. When we questioned why those items cost so much compared to the other plants on the list, the landscaper explained that the supplier did not grow those items, but had to buy them from other growers in order to bid the whole job. The landscaper was willing to pay the higher price on those items for the convenience of getting all or the majority of the material in one delivery from one source.

JOBBERS

The convenience of finding all you need from one source has also created a place in the industry for a different type of marketer called a jobber. A jobber's talent is locating plants for clients, not growing. He takes landscape plans filled with divergent plants and collects all those plants from various sources, usually looking for the best price. The jobber either resells the plants or takes a commission for the complete package. Landscapers frequently use jobbers to save themselves considerable time. Jobbers can also contract with growers to produce plants for them, which they distribute throughout the industry serving as middlemen between growers and buyers.

The best way to find a jobber is to check the nursery license roster for those who have listed themselves as jobbers. You can also get names from landscapers who are using their services. By making yourself known to such people, you can increase your sales potential and also gain some valuable information on what types of plants to grow. Jobbers are always looking for sources, but not competing for the market by growing plants themselves.

OTHER BACKYARD GROWERS

In the course of your prospecting, you may run across landscapers or other small backyard growers similar to yourself who are growing some plant material. They may be interested in buying liners or gallons for shifting into larger sizes. In dealing with like-minded individuals, a certain amount of creative marketing is possible. Trading becomes a very interesting option that can be used advantageously by both parties, exchanging some of your overstock for some different varieties of theirs. For example, if you have 500 daylilies which are selling more slowly than you expected, you may find it advantageous to trade 200 of them for 200 agapanthus. This can reduce the glut of daylilies by 200 plants and increase your inventory variety with 200 agapanthus. You have no fewer plants, but you may find it easier to sell 300 daylilies and 200 agapanthus than all 500 daylilies.

How do you find other small growers? Most are not in the yellow pages, but they should be in the directory listing all the licensed nurseries in the state and the types of material which they produce. You will find this information well worth having.

LANDSCAPERS

Marketing to independent landscapers who are not part of a nursery operation is significantly different from selling to retail nurseries. Landscapers are installers of plants, not retailers of landscape material. They do not maintain an inventory nor do they need plants until they have won a bid for installation. When they undertake a large commercial project, they are following a plan drawn by a landscape architect and approved by the planning commission. If you have been watching a commercial site develop with the hopes of selling your plants when it comes time to landscape, you might be disappointed. In most cases there is little opportunity for the small grower to sell material to landscapers on large commercial projects already underway since the material usually is contracted long in advance. The site may be of value to you only as a source for used containers. Even so, when you are buying containers you have the landscaper's ear and it never hurts to ask if he needs anything for the project. He may have trouble finding certain plants on the plan or there may have been last minute changes. Opportunities do exist. If he needs nothing for his current project, ask about the other projects coming up. The costs landscapers can best control are the prices paid for materials, so finding plants at a better price translates to an improvement in the profit picture. Lower pricing is always a strong motivator, but landscapers want to be sure the quality is there too. Be prepared to show them samples.

Commercial landscapers always need plants. Buying containers from them opens the door to doing future selling business with them. Suggest that they provide you with the cans as a down payment for contract growing some of the plants for their upcoming projects. Not every job needs the plants the next week; some have six to eight months lead-time, which gives you enough time to grow some of the material called for on the project plan. This can be a very successful relationship for both parties. For example, commercial landscapers who specialize in freeway landscaping or reclamation projects may need a certain variety of plant not easily found. They may only get it in sufficient quantity if they have it contract grown.

Some landscapers draw the plans they use on projects and have favorite plants which they use again and again in their designs. They may be able to estimate how many they will use in a year, but since they cannot really be sure that they will need the plants they are not likely to commit to specific numbers. When contractors landscape single family homes in new tracts, they usually have more flexibility in the plant material they can use. Their guidelines may be only a certain number of shrubs in #1s or #5s and trees in #5s or #15s. The landscapers may be willing to work with the types of plants you grow, if you in turn are willing to work with them on the prices. Pricing is the best incentive for them to do business with you.

Another source of sales in the landscaping industry is the landscape maintenance gardener. Most of these people are independent small business operators specializing in mowing and trimming existing landscaping, but occasionally they have projects for which they need plants. They usually buy from retail nurseries, since they are not buying in wholesale quantities. The retail nursery customarily gives maintenance landscapers a professional discount of 20% on the retail price of green goods, that is, plant material. If they have the opportunity to purchase from you at true wholesale prices, it will lead to a significant increase in your profit picture as well as theirs, and assure you a steady flow of business. They seldom have to follow a landscape plan and they often have control over the types of plants they install. They probably will work with what you have rather than buy more expensive plants elsewhere. In order to attract this business, you have to grow a varied inventory so that they can find a selection of different plants.

There is another opportunity to do business with landscapers which is not to be overlooked: trading plants for empty cans. Although no money changes hands, trading is sometimes actually better. To generate cash to buy cans takes time and effort finding a buyer for the plants. Trading for cans eliminates this step; you find a buyer and a can supply in the same place.

To reach a large number of landscapers, consult the listing of landscape contractors in the yellow pages for a list of your potential clients and their addresses. Make up a flier listing what you have currently available for sale and either mail it or deliver it in person. It is always a good idea to follow up with a phone call.

SELLING TO THE PUBLIC: SELLING FROM YOUR HOME

In the above discussion on selling to retailers and landscapers, you are usually making sales calls at their place of business. This is typical of wholesale selling, but you may prefer to take on the role of retailer and sell your plants directly to the public where you can obtain a higher price.

Most direct sales to individuals are on a cash basis so you are not concerned with billing and deferred payment, but you must consider what kind of plant guarantee you offer the public. Retail guarantees vary throughout the industry. At the least, a retailer warrants that the plants are in good condition at the time of sale. Some stores give sixty or ninety day guarantees and other stores give unconditional one year guarantees. You have to decide for yourself how you warrant your plants. People do not want to take chances, but the truth of the matter is that usually it is the customer's fault that a plant dies and it is usually a water related problem, either too much or too little. If you are selling at wholesale prices, it makes little sense to guarantee anything to individuals, especially since a retailer does not expect any warranty from you. If you are selling at full retail, then there is room in the price for a guarantee. Remember, a guarantee is an insurance policy, and if you give one, charge for it.

There are basically two ways to access your retail consumers: you can have them come to you or you can go to them. Zoning regulations determine what is possible for you. In commercial and farm zones, few restrictions are placed on selling plants from your property; even roadside stands may be permitted. We begin our discussion with those properties where zoning allows you to retail from your land.

There are several things to consider before you attempt to attract customers. How much time do you want to give to the public? Do you want regular business hours? How much privacy are you willing to give up to open your property to customers? The advantages to retailing from your own home are that you have few of the direct overhead expenses of the typical retailer. You are not paying for expensive advertising, separate rent on the business location or extra utilities; but once you expose yourself to the public, there is the additional consideration of liability insurance to cover any injury which may occur on your property.

Once you have addressed these issues and have decided how to proceed, your next step is to serve notice to the public that you are there. How? Advertising is the natural first response to this question. A sign, conspicuously placed, is one of the most obvious ways to advertise your business. Decide whether you want your sign to be permanent or temporary. A permanent sign implies that you are open for business year-round, and can attract a certain number of people who are just curious. It is best to have your operating hours and seasons clearly stated on the sign. A temporary sign, such as a simple A-frame, is preferable if you want to attract business only at certain times or seasons.

The traditional mass media advertising in the newspapers or on the airwaves used by the large garden centers is not a viable option for a grower who has only a small inventory, nor is it necessary. That you do not need such advertising to prosper is the main thesis of the book *Marketing Without Advertising* by Michael Phillips and Salli Rasberry. First and foremost, they contend that media advertising is not cost effective for a small business, nor does it attract a loyal customer base. The types of ads that work best for small businesses are what they termed "listings." These are simple advertising notices placed where people are looking for such notices.

The Yellow Page ad is such a notice. If customers are looking for plants, they will consult the heading for Nurseries. Most full-time businesses want to be listed in the Yellow Pages since they are an excellent source of customers as well as being a fairly inexpensive way to advertise. Beware of listing your own residential phone unless you really want to tie up that line with business calls or miss potential calls because you are using the line in conversation with friends or family. If you are listing your business in the phone book, you should have a separate business line and perhaps an answering machine to take the calls. But remember, as with the case of the permanent sign, the Yellow Page ad implies a year-round business, so you may be fielding calls for months when you have nothing to sell. A listing in the Yellow Pages may not be for you.

More temporary notices of plants for sale can be placed in the small local advertising papers often called Magic Ads or Penny Savers, which are considerably less expensive than regular newspapers. Fliers and business cards can also be placed in locations where potential customers look for such notices. If you sell trees, you might have fliers at stores which sell supplies to arborists. In rural areas, a notice at a feed store for pasture or screening trees may be a valuable listing. Notices of plants for sale posted at hardware stores or landscape supply houses which sell garden supplies, but have no nursery of their own, may catch the eyes of their customers.

Write your ad in such a way as to prescreen your customer response. This can save you a great deal of unnecessary phone time. If you just list your nursery business name and phone number, you will get calls for any types of plants that nurseries sell. If you advertise trees for sale, your ad response should be limited to customers who are interested in buying trees. If you advertise birch trees, your response should be limited to those who want birch trees.

Once you begin to attract your initial customers, you are in a position to cultivate the most effective form of advertising for a small business, that is, the personal recommendation. Phillips and Rasberry (2.1) termed the personal recommendation "the first choice in marketing." They assert, "In our view, promoting personal recommendations is a superior, yet often overlooked, strategy to attract and keep customers." The way you service each and every customer reflects on your future recommendations. Plants are very visible purchases which people take home and install in their yards, usually with other neighbors watching. Plants and landscaping are frequent topics of conversation, especially in new neighborhoods. And people do love to tell other people about good deals they found.

In striving to earn more personal recommendations from customers, there is one more thing to consider beyond the impression that you and your product make. When delivering plants out to other locations, your customer does not see the environment from which the plants are shipped. But if your customers come to your home, the general appearance of your business makes an impression. Cleanliness is not an easy proposition for a business which has dirt as one of the major ingredients of its product. But Phillips and Rasberry (3.4) point out that "Cleanliness is crucially important in all business, and is perceived by the public as a measure of management competence." A few weeds people can live with, but what kind of impression does it make if everything is filled with weeds and dead material remains in the beds?

GARAGE SALES

If you are in a residential area where your zoning and business license prohibit retail traffic to your house, you may still be allowed to have a certain number of garage sales each year. Hundreds of dollars can be generated from a one day sale, and if you only have a small number of plants, it is the perfect way to sell them. You can also take your plants to garage sales which friends and family hold. Our relatives ask us to bring plants to their sales, because flowering plants attract customers and induce people to stop and look at things.

TAKING THE PRODUCT TO THE PUBLIC

The second option in selling to the public is to take the material directly to the public. Zoning which restricts any kind of retail traffic to your home may, for the most part, force you to market your product away from the home. Even those of you in the country who can have customers to your property may find that it is better to take the product to the customers rather than wait for them to come to you. Some growers have marketed thousands of dollars worth of plants by taking truckloads of them into new subdivisions and soliciting door-to-door. Others simply set plants out at roadside corners. Another option is to take your plants to a farmers market or flea market. Additional licenses may be necessary for these activities, so check with the city or county.

CERTIFIED FARMERS MARKETS

Certified farmers markets are set up especially for the small growers of fruits and vegetables who need an outlet for their fresh produce without meeting the size requirements that restrict the sale of such produce in the larger commercial markets. Certified markets have also become outlets for organically grown produce often unavailable in grocery stores. Since the small scale growers of plant material are in a related agricultural field, they have been accommodated within this framework, and it is a market especially appropriate for herb growers. The major condition for participation in the certified farmers market is that the product be from your own production, not purchased from others for resale. This does not mean that you cannot buy liners and shift up material which you grow to larger sizes, but you cannot buy market-ready plants and simply resell them. Just what restrictions apply depend on the agricultural rules in your area, on the operator of the market and on the other vendors. Membership in a grower's association may be required by some certified markets.

Plants sold at a produce market.

FLEA MARKETS

The flea market is related to the farmers market and sometimes includes a farmers market, but it attracts a wider range of customers, not just produce buyers. It is especially useful if you prefer to have your garage sale away from your home. This avenue of marketing has many advantages and offers small growers great flexibility. First, it offers a public location which can be rented by the day. Usually the days are limited to the weekends, which are typically the days on which people shop for plants. The flea market provides a public business location available to you when you want it with no long term lease commitment, no utilities and no maintenance. You only have to rent space one day at a time, usually without making a reservation, so it easy to avoid the bad weather days. You get high customer traffic without advertising expense. However, selling at such markets is not totally risk-free since there are indemnification and insurance clauses in the rental agreements for spaces at both farmers markets and flea markets.

Doing business at a flea market is more like the old days when there were no fixed prices on merchandise and the merchant and customer negotiated the price. Fixed pricing has become a way of life in our everyday shopping and in a retail store we would not think of making an offer on a shirt when we go to the counter. We either wait for it to go on sale or we pay the regular price. Things are changing a bit now with many stores guaranteeing the lowest price and promising to beat any advertised price. The bargain price has always been synonymous with the flea market and part of the fun of shopping the market is negotiating for the lowest price on everything. To many people the listed price doesn't mean anything except that we only go down from here.

Pricing is a foremost consideration in selling at the flea market, and it is something for which you will have to develop a feel. People go to flea markets to find a bargain. In our earlier discussion on how to determine wholesale pricing when selling to retailers, we suggested that you consult the catalogues of other wholesale growers. Their prices set the upper limit for what you can ask from the retailer. To determine the upper limit the flea market customer will pay, you must visit the retail nurseries to determine where they have priced their plants. The majority of people who buy plants at a flea market have a good idea what the prices are at a local discount nursery. This does not mean that you have to have the absolute lowest price in order to sell at the flea market, but it is one of the strongest motivators in getting people to buy.

Plants displayed for sale at a flea market.

You have to realize that even if you have priced your plants at true bargain prices, some customers think that they can get them for less because, "This is the flea market." Does this mean that you have to put a higher price on your plant and negotiate every single sale? No. If you offer your plants at true bargain prices, most people will pay the prices asked. They may ask if you will take less, but that is force of habit and it comforts them knowing that they did not pay more than they had to. Remember, however, when you are selling to the public, you are taking on the additional role of retailer. To compensate yourself for that extra marketing time you should set your prices higher than the wholesale prices which a retail nursery or landscaper will pay you, but to assure yourself greater marketability, keep your prices close to the discount stores.

Your best prospects for realizing the highest price come when your plants are in bloom. Remember our earlier advice on what to grow. When in doubt, grow something that flowers. Flowers have an effect on people's sensitivities that softens even the most hardened bargain hunters. A pretty flower sells an ugly plant. The period of time when the plant is blooming is your best window of opportunity to market it to the public and to obtain the best price. Many plants only attract attention for the one short season they are in bloom and go unnoticed and unwanted for the rest of the year. Frequently that is when the retail nursery puts the plant on sale. If you plan on using the flea market only a few times a year, wait for the season when you can maximize the plants' most appealing features, whether it is the blooming season or the change of color in the fall.

While targeting the peak marketing time can maximize your profit on desirable material, the flea market is also a good place to unload the plants which you are unable to sell elsewhere. These plants may be ones which missed the prime market season, and you do not want to hold them until next year, or they may be overstock material which is glutting the market. These are the kinds of items that the retailers put on sale as clearance items and low pricing becomes the main strategy for moving this type of merchandise. You may also have plants which the nursery industry would consider substandard, and these plants can best be sold at the flea market. While all these plants are perfectly healthy, they are difficult to sell due to imperfections. Many retail nurseries do not even offer such plants for sale, preferring to dump them into the garbage and thereby maintain their reputation for quality. At the flea market, price often takes precedence over quality, especially if the price has been significantly reduced in order to compensate for a plant's deficiencies. For example, you may have a tree which has grown a crooked trunk. A retail nursery does not want it in its sales area because customers will not pay $25.00 for such a misshapen tree. However, you may find someone at the flea market who wants to put some trees in a pasture, but does not want to invest any significant money in something which the animals may eat or break. It is not a concern if it is a little crooked as long as it makes shade for the cows. A price of $5.00 looks better to the customer than $25.00 and to you $5.00 looks better than throwing it into the garbage. The flea market then is a good place to obtain some salvage value from your more unsuccessful work.

While trying to liquidate some lower grade material, I discovered that it is possible to price your product too low. Once I had some thujas in five gallon containers which were not retail nursery quality and never would be. I decided to get rid of them for anything I could over the $2.50 cash investment I had in each plant. So I decided that a price of $3.50, instead of the $6.00 I had been asking, would be such a great bargain that I would sell them very quickly. But $3.50 only made people suspicious and I found myself answering the all too common question, "What's wrong with them?" I sold a few, but was very disappointed. I then raised the price to $5.00. It was clear to the customer that there were deficiencies in the plants; they were ugly, but they would grow out of it. It is just this kind of thinking that motivates someone to try to get a better deal. I eventually sold all the plants by negotiating the price with any interested customer and usually the plants sold for $4.00 on an offer. Too good a bargain can activate suspicions that something must be really wrong with the plant, or it wouldn't be that cheap.

One drawback to selling plants at flea markets is that the customer does not want to carry heavy plants around while looking for other bargains. Come prepared with some kind of bags, boxes, dolly or cart so that they can get the plants to their cars or trucks. If you lend the cart, it is always wise to take a deposit.

Do not overlook the advertising potential of the flea market or the farmers market. Do not think in terms of selling just the plants that you brought that day. There will be some customers who may be interested in buying large quantities of plants at a later time to use in their landscape plan when the pool is finished. Not everyone is ready to use plants the day you are there. You should pass out business cards or fliers to all the people with whom you come in contact. We found fliers to be our best advertising tool. There were many days when the sales from the fliers far exceeded the amount of material I could haul to the market in a pickup load. Even if you do not want people to come to your home, you still have the option of delivering material out to the customer. Take orders whenever possible.

SALES TAX

It is important to note that in any type of selling directly to the public you have to collect sales tax. When you price material at garage sales and flea markets, you have to include the tax in your price because these customers do not expect or intend to pay any extra money for tax. If you quote a price of $5.00, that is the full price to them, but the state expects its share of the transaction. It is your responsibility to collect and pay sales tax. This means that your net from a $5.00 sale is reduced by the sales tax. If your sales tax is 6%, then your $5.00 price represents 106% of the retail price, that is, the price of the plant plus the sales tax. To determine the retail price of the plant you must divide the $5.00 price by 1.06 which gives you $4.72; the $4.72 is yours, the $.28 is the state's sales tax.

RESELLING MATERIAL NOT OF YOUR OWN PRODUCTION

There is one other potential for profit not to be overlooked when selling directly to the public. You have the same opportunities as any retailer to buy what someone else has grown and resell it at a profit without adding any of your own growing time. This kind of selling can be a separate business for you all in itself, but we discuss it here only as a side line in conjunction with growing material. In choosing what to resell you are simply using the same skills employed in choosing what to buy for transplanting. When you find well-priced sources for your canning material, you have also found well-priced plants for resale.

The safest way to invest in plants for resale is to have a double purpose. If you do not sell them, transplant them into larger containers and grow them into larger profits. For the most part, we are talking about one gallon plants and bareroot which can be moved up into fives, rather than five gallon plants which are basically at the end of the move-up line. For example, we bought 100 azaleas at a price of $2.05 each with the intention of quickly reselling them at $3.50. We had none of our own and their flowers offered more variety to what we were trying to sell from our own production. We were confident that the flowers would sell the plants, but one week after we took delivery, a local chain store advertised azaleas on sale for $1.88. This, of course, made it difficult to sell azaleas at $3.50. By the time the store sale was over and people were willing to spend $3.50 again, a number of the plants were done blooming, making them much less marketable. These were canned into five gallons and held until they came into bloom again and sold for a much higher price. Those that sold for $3.50 while in bloom paid for the ones we canned into fives.

Bareroot selling offers excellent profit potential. Fruit trees are commonly sold bareroot, as are roses, and many people are familiar with buying these plants this way. However, the areas of bareroot shade trees, shrubs and vines are no longer heavily exploited by many retail stores, especially when it comes to the smaller seedlings. There is a very wide variety of material available at very low prices. For example, 2-3' bareroot seedling lilacs can be purchased for about $1.50 each in quantities of 100. Similar lilacs sold by a retail-ready bareroot grower sell wholesale for $5.00 each in quantities of ten. The difference of $3.50 between growers can easily be translated to retail profit, but you have to buy 100 lilacs to get the price and that may be more than you want or need. Offer the bareroot lilacs for sale at $4.00 each. That is a very attractive price, already $1.00 below the other grower's $5.00 wholesale price. You make $2.50 per plant, which is $1.00 more than the nurseryman who grew it. If you sell half as bareroots for $4.00 each, you take in $200.00, which pays for all 100 plants and the canning cost of the remaining fifty. You now have a crop of 50 five gallon lilacs sitting in your field with no cash invested.

This is just one example, but the bareroot season offers many such opportunities and is one of the more interesting avenues to pursue because none of the discount stores are geared to do this kind of business, preferring instead to buy their bareroot in packages. If you are selling directly to the public, you can sell a portion or all of what you buy before you have to containerize the plants. The larger size seedlings tend to be the most marketable and in many cases we have seen that the price differential for larger sizes is not substantial. For example, a 2-3' branched lilac at $1.50 is only $.90 more than a small 6-12" lilac. The larger plant makes a better presentation. Customers like to get the largest plant possible for the money. This market is relatively unexplored, and it is possible for you to identify and exploit a niche by selling material in sizes not frequently found in the retail nurseries.

If you are only familiar with the packaged bareroot offered for retail sale, you may be wondering how in the world you can sell unpackaged bareroot plants at a flea market. Don't they dry out? When we discussed how to handle bareroot upon delivery, one of the methods suggested was to put the plants into a #15 container and cover the roots with compost to keep them moist. This works for seedlings and sizes up to 3/4" trees. The #15 container is moveable and easily loaded onto a pickup and off to the flea market it goes. If you break your bundles apart and separate and sort out the plants, you can arrange them in the containers so that they can be easily pulled out. You may want to use sawdust instead of a soil that tends to pack down. You should be able to pull the plants out easily without breaking or tearing the roots.

When customers choose their plants, you then have to put them into some kind of bag to prevent the roots from drying out. Plastic grocery bags work well, being large enough to cover many of the root systems. You can save bags all year until bareroot season. When you bag the plants, add a little moist compost or sawdust around the roots. Now your customer is taking the plant home in a plastic bag, just like the commercially bagged material. Well almost, for the pretty picture is still missing. Pictures are useful in selling dormant bareroot plants. A laminated picture of the plant on a sign in the container or one in a catalogue which you can show to your customers is one of your best marketing tools. Most mail order material is sold bareroot. The pictures in the catalogues sell the plants sight unseen, so do not underestimate the value of pictures which show your customers what the plants will look like with leaves and flowers. Keep in mind that not everyone understands how bareroot plants are sold. Some wonder if the plants are really alive and others invariably think that your pricing is for all the plants in the barrel. Make sure you put the word "each" with your price and be prepared to explain how the plants are sold and how they are to be handled.

Selling bareroot plants in the winter is a way to exploit the market during one of the slowest seasons of the year. You can sell enough to pay for your entire order and have material left over to containerize and sell for higher profits later.

OTHER MARKETS

There are many other marketing possibilities for growers of plant material. Utility districts, park districts, school districts, state and federal reclamation projects, home owner associations, golf courses and cemetery districts all buy plant material, and this does not exhaust the list of potential markets. Many of the government projects go out to bid with public notice and invitations to bid. You may not be in a position to perform on the whole bid, but you may win part or you may be able to sell material to the contractors who do win the bids.

An industrious individual can discover new markets suited to particular circumstances. Unexpected opportunities to sell your material will develop after you have been in business for a while and have made more contacts. Word of mouth is one of your most valuable sales tools, but this only comes with customer satisfaction. The more customers you deal with over the years, the more your name is passed around and the easier the whole selling process becomes. But first you need something to sell, so now it's time to get growing!

APPENDIX ONE

NURSERYMEN ASSOCIATIONS

United States

American Association of Nurserymen
1250 I Street NW Suite 500
Washington, DC 20005-3994
(202) 789-2900
FAX (202) 789-1893

Alabama Nurserymen's Association
PO Box 9
Auburn, AL 36831-0009
(205) 821-5148
FAX (205) 821-5148 #11

Arizona Nursery Association
1430 West Broadway #A-125
Tempe, AZ 85210
(602) 966-1610
FAX (602) 966-0923

Arkansas Nurserymen's Association
PO Box 55295
Little Rock, AR 72225
(501) 225 0029

California Association of Nurserymen
4620 Northgate Blvd. Suite 155
Sacramento, CA 95834
(916) 567-0200
(800) 748-6214
FAX (916) 567-0505

Colorado Nurserymen's Association
9101 E. Kenyon Ave., Suite 3000
Denver, CO 80237
(303) 770-3343
FAX (303) 770-1812

Connecticut Nurserymen's Association
and
Eastern Regional Nurserymen's Association
PO Box 117
Vernon, CT 06066
(203) 872-2095
FAX (203) 872-6596

Delaware Association of Nurserymen
Plant Science Department, University of
Delaware
Newark, DE 19717
(302) 451-2531

Florida Nurserymen and Growers Association
5401 Kirkman Road, Suite 650
Orlando, FL 32819-7942
(407) 345-8137
FAX (407) 351 2610

Georgia Green Industry Association
PO Box 369
Epworth, GA 30451
(706) 492-4664
FAX (706) 492-4668

Hawaii Association of Nurserymen
PO Box 293
Honolulu, HI 96809
(808) 833-3369

Idaho Nursery Association
2104 Floating Feather Road
Eagle, ID 83616
(800) 462-4769

Illinois Nurserymen's Association
1717 South Fifth Street
Springfield, IL 62703
(217) 525-6222
FAX (217) 525-6257

Indiana Association of Nurserymen
202 East 650 North
West Lafayette, IN 47906
(317) 497-1100
FAX (317 463-0190

Iowa Nurserymen's Association
7261 NW 21st Street
Ankeny, IA 50021
(515) 289-1790

Kansas Association of Nurserymen
411 Poplar
Wamego, KS 66547
(913) 456-2066

Kentucky Nurserymen's Association
701 Baxter Avenue
Louisville, KY 40204
(502) 451-5630
FAX (502) 429-6205

Louisiana Association of Nurserymen
4560 Essen Lane
Baton Rouge, LA 70809
(504) 766-3471
FAX (504) 766-3664

Maine Landscape and Nursery Association
PST/SMTC
South Portland, ME 04106
(207) 767-9646
FAX (207) 767-2731

Maryland Nurserymen's Association
PO Box 432
Perry Hall, MD 21128
(410) 256-1799
FAX (410) 256-2208

Massachusetts Nurserymen's Association
PO Box 706
Leominster, MA 01453
(508) 534-1775

Michigan Nursery and Landscape Association
819 North Washington Avenue, Suite 2
Lansing, MI 48840
(517) 487-1282
FAX (517) 487-0969

Minnesota Nursery and Landscape
Association
PO Box 10307
St. Paul, MN 55113
(612) 633-4987
FAX (612) 633-4986

Montana Association of Nurserymen
PO Box 1871
Bozeman, MT 59771-1871
(406) 586-6042
FAX (406) 585-7474

Mississippi Nurserymen's Association
PO Box 5385
Mississippi State, MS 39762
(601) 325-1682
FAX (601) 325-8407

Missouri Association of Nurserymen
and
Western Association of Nurserymen
Rt 1 Box 175
Clarksdale, MO 64430
(816) 369-2005

Nebraska Association of Nurserymen
PO Box 80177
Lincoln, NE 68501
(402) 476-3852
FAX (816) 369-3000

Nevada Nurserymen's Association
4850 Kilda Circle
Las Vegas, NV 89112
(702) 361-3501

New Hampshire Plant Growers Association
56 Leavitt Road
Hampton, NH 03842
(603) 862-1074

New Jersey Nursery and Landscape
Association
605 Farnsworth Ave.
Bordentown, NJ 08505
(609) 291-7070
FAX (609) 291-1121

New Mexico Association of Nursery
Industries
PO Box 667
Estancia, NM 87016

New York Nursery/Landscape Association
PO Box 657
Baldwinsville, NY 13027
(800) 647-0384
FAX (315) 699-3995

North Carolina Association of Nurserymen
PO Box 400
Knightdale, NC 27545-0400
(919) 266-3322
FAX (919) 266-2137

North Dakota Nursery and Greenhouse
Association
PO Box 10444
Fargo, ND 58106
(701) 232-0215

Ohio Nurserymen's Association
2021 East Dublin-Granville Road, Suite 185
Columbus, OH 43229-3530
(800) 852-5062
FAX (614) 431-8032

Oklahoma State Nurserymen's Association
400 North Portland
Oklahoma City, OK 73107
(405) 942-5276

Oregon Association of Nurserymen
2780 SE Harrison Street, Suite 102
Milwaukie, OR 97222-7584
(503) 653-8733
(800) 342-6401
FAX (503) 653-1528

Pennsylvania Nurserymen's Association
1924 North Second Street
Harrisburg, PA 17102-2209
(717) 238-1673
FAX (717) 238-1675

Rhode Island Nurserymen's Association
64 Bittersweet Drive
Seekonk,MA 02771
(508) 761-9260

South Carolina Nurserymen's Association
809 Sunset Drive
Greenwood, SC 29646-1117
(803) 223-7278
FAX (803) 223-5785

South Dakota Nurserymen's Association
RR 5, Box 392A
Huron, SD 57350
(605) 352-4414

Southern Nurserymen's Association
1000 Johson Ferry Rd, Suite E-130
Marietta, GA 30068
(404) 973-9026
FAX (404) 973-9097

Tennessee Nurserymen's Association
PO Box 57
McMinnville, TN 37110
(615) 473-3951

Texas Association of Nurserymen
7730 South I-H 35
Austin, TX 78745-6621
(512) 280-5182
FAX (512) 280-3012

Utah Association of Nurserymen and Landscape Contractors
470 E. 3900 So. , Suite 108
Salt Lake City, UT 84107
(801) 288-8858

Vermont Plantsmen's Association
RR4, Box 2287
Montpelier, VT 05602
(802) 223-2944

Virginia Nurserymen's Association
383 Coal Hollow Road
Christiansburg, VA 24073-6721
(703) 382-0943
FAX (703) 382-2716

Washington State Nursery and Landscape
Association
PO Box 670
Sumner, WA 98390
(206) 863-4482
FAX (206) 863-6732

West Virginia Nurserymen's Association
965 National Rd.
Wheeling, WV 26003
(304) 233-4140

Wisconsin Nurserymen's Association
9910 West Layton Avenue
Greenfield, WI 53228
(414) 529-4705
FAX (414) 529-4722

Canadian Associations

Atlantic Provinces Nursery Trades
Association
PO Box 58
Mt. Uniacke, Hants County, Nova Scotia
Canada, B0N 1Z0
(902) 866-2073

British Columbia Nursery Trades Association
#107 - 14914 104th Avenue
Surrey, British Columbia
Canada V3R 1M7
(604) 585-2225
FAX (604) 585-3496

Landscape Alberta Nursery Trades
Association
7603 13th Avenue
Edmonton, Alberta
Canada T6K 2T5
(403) 463-7485

Landscape Manitoba Nursery Trades
Association
808 Muriel Street
Winnipeg, Manitoba
Canada, R2Y 0Y3
(2f04) 889-5981

Landscape Ontario Horticultural Trades
Association
1293 Matheson Boulevard
Mississauga, Ontario
Canada L4W 1R1
(416) 629-1184
FAX (416) 629-4438

Saskatchewan Nursery Trades Association
256 Habkirk Dr.
Regina, Saskatchewan
Canada F4F 5X8
(306) 359-3013

APPENDIX TWO

WHOLESALE NURSERY SUPPLIERS

Alabama

Alabama Nursery Supply (BWI)
8900 Muffet Road
Semmes, AL 36575
 205-649-0086

Cassco
PO Box 3508
Montgomery, AL 36109-0508
 205-272-2140

George Dodd Nursery Supply
PO Box 86
Semmes, AL 36575
 205-649-6650

Montgomery Seed & Supply
PO Box 349
Montgomery, AL 36101-0349

Terra International
PO Box 7064
Dothan, AL 36302

Terra International
25187 Brownsferry Road
Madison, AL 35758

Terra International
Route 1, Sanborne
Summerdale, AL 36580

Universal Seed & Supply
Birmingham   205-252-9537

Alaska

Alaska Mill & Feed
114 North Orca
Anchorage, AK 99501
907-279-4519

V.F. Grace, Inc.
605 East 13th Street
Anchorage, AK 99501
907-272-6431

Arizona

Garden West Dist.
2529 West Jackson
Phoenix, AZ 85005
602-272-5508

Snyder Turf Supply
6002 East Delcoa Drive
Phoenix, AZ 85254
602-948-9107

Target Specialty Products
4865 South 36th Street
Phoenix, AZ 85040
602-437-4642

Triple A Fertilizer
8665 South Alvernon Street
Tucson, AZ 85726
602-574-0040

UHS, Inc.
4429 North Highway Drive
Tucson, AZ 85705
602-293-4330

185

Wilbur Ellis Company
11411 East Chandler Heights
Chandler, AZ 85249
602-895-7699

California

Agri Chemical & Supply
2002 Oceanside Blvd.
Oceanside, CA 92054
619-757-1848

Agricultural Supply, Inc.
1435 Simpson Way
Escondido, CA 92025
619-741-0066

Agro Mex
2310 Marconi Court
San Diego, CA 92073
619-661-6660

American Horticultural Supply, Inc.
Camarillo   805-389-6528
Toll Free   800-247-1184

Associated Chemicals
Copperswitch & Castroville
Salinas, CA 93901
408-422-6452

Automatic Rain Company
1880 Arnold Industrial Place
Concord, CA 94520
510-825-3344

Automatic Rain Company
349 West Bedford Avenue
Fresno, CA 93711
209-431-8007

Automatic Rain Company
4060 Campbell Avenue
Menlo Park, CA 94026
408-323-5161

Automatic Rain Company
3065 North Highway 59
Merced, CA 95340
209-383-3330

Automatic Rain Company
3229 California Blvd.
Napa, CA 94558
707-255-7575

Automatic Rain Company
1064 Serpentine Lane
Pleasanton, CA 94566
510-484-1170

Automatic Rain Company
560 Brunken Avenue
Salinas, CA 93901
408-757-1045

Automatic Rain Company
63 Larkspur Street
San Rafael, CA 94901
415-454-4313

Automatic Rain Company
3370 Keller Street
Santa Clara, CA 95054
408-988-7593

Automatic Rain Company
238-A Todd Road
Santa Rosa, CA 95407
707-584-7272

Automatic Rain Company
1232 Callen Street
Vacaville, CA 95688
707-447-7773

Butlers Mill, Inc.
5180 Naranja Street
San Diego, CA 92114
619-263-6181

Calif. Ag Resources
PO Box 2008
Oxnard, CA 93034
805-487-0696

Calif. Chrysanthemum
788 San Antonio Road
Palo Alto, CA 94303
408-494-1451

Central Garden Supply
PO Box 899
Lafayette, CA 94549
510-283-4994

Chem Tec
3155 Southgate Lane
Chico, CA 95928
919-345-6148

Crop Production Services
PO Box 2509
Bakersfield, CA 93301
805-633-5733

Crop Production Services
4075 Dufau Road
Oxnard, CA 93033
805-488-3646

Crop Production Services
2622 - 3rd Street
Riverside, CA 92507
909-686-3236

Crop Production Services
PO Box 5188
Stockton, CA 95205
209-466-2041

Crop Produuction Services
1276 Halyard Drive
West Sacramento, CA 95691
916-372-7011

Farm Supply
675 Tank Farm Road
San Luis Obispo, CA 93406
805-543-3751

Farm Supply
125 South Blosser Road
Santa Maria, CA 93456
805-922-2737

Gro Max Company
158 Central Avenue, Suite 2
Salinas, CA 93901
408-757-2494

Hughson Chemical Company
6800 East Whitemore Avenue
Hughson, CA 95326
209-883-4025

Hydro-Scape Products
5805 Kearny Villa Road
San Diego, CA 92123
619-560-6611

Independent Greenhouse Services
Santa Maria   805-481-1289

Kuida Ag Supply
635 South Sanborn Road #19
Salinas, CA 93901
408-758-9914

Kuida Farm Supply
711 South Grand Avenue
Santa Ana, CA 92715
714-835-6106

L&L Nursery Supply
5350 "G" Street
Chino, CA 91710
714-591-0461

Louisiana Pacific Timber
1508 Carnell Road
Trinidad, CA 95570
707-677-0911

McCalif Growers Supply
PO Box 310
Ceres, CA 95307
Ceres   209-538-1997
Toll Free   800-234-4559
Vista   619-727-7190
Toll Free   800-677-3824

McConkey Company
12321 Western Avenue
Garden Grove, CA 92641
 714-894-0581

North California Fert.
1158 Berryessa Road
San Jose, CA 95133
408-453-7907

Nurserymen's Exchange
Half Moon Bay 415-726-6361

Orange County Farm Supply
1826 West Chapman Avenue
Orange, CA 92668
714-972-6500

Paramount Perlite
16326 Illinois Street
Paramount, CA 90723
213-633-1291

ReForestation Tech.
35 Questa Vista Drive
Monterey, CA 93940
408-655-5309

Robinson Fertilizer Company
1460 North Red Gum Road
Anaheim, CA 90701
310-865-9541

Seeley Wholesale Dist.
now Western Farm Service
210 North Thorne Avenue
Fresno, CA 93706
209-442-8118
800-543-8564

Sierra Pacific Turf Supply
510 Salmar Avenue
Campbell, CA 95008
408-374-4700

Sparetime Supply
208 East San Francisco Avenue
Willits, CA 94590
707-459-6791

Speedling, Incorporated
Nipomo   805-489-8500
Toll Free   800-557-8500
San Juan Batista 408-623-4432

Sprinkler Irrigation
6450-B Trinity Court
Dublin, CA 94568
510-829-6040

Sprinkler Irrigation
701 Kearney Avenue #8
Modesto, CA 95350
209-349-0316

Sprinkler Irrigation
865 Sweeter Avenue
Novato, CA 94947
415-892-4680

Sprinkler Irrigation
130-A South Buchanan Street
Pacheco, CA 94553
510-680-7629

Sprinkler Irrigation
6500 Elvas Avenue
Sacramento, CA 95819
916-452-8041

Sprinkler Irrigation
1158 - 19th Street
San Mateo, CA 94403
415-349-0316

Sprinkler Irrigation
180 Sebastopol Road
Santa Rosa, CA 95407
707-526-1171

Sprinkler Irrigation
4045 Sunset Lane
Shingle Springs, CA 95862
916-677-0357

Target Specialty Products
17710 Studebaker Road
Cerritos, CA 90701
310-865-9541

Target Specialty Products
2478 Sunnyside Avenue
Fresno, CA 93727
209-291-7740

Target Specialty Products
80 North 10th Street
San Jose, CA 95112
408-293-6032

T&C Supplies, Inc.
Gilroy   408-848-2448

Turf Tech
5600 Imhoff Drive #G
Concord, CA 94520
510-225-1668

Turf Tech
10210 Systems Parkway #30
Sacramento, CA 95827
916-369-2891

United Horticultural Supply
37343 Blacow Road
Fremont, CA 94538
510-792-4031

Western Farm Service
33 South Kellog Avenue
Goleta, CA 93017
805-964-3501

Western Farm Service
1015 East Wooley Road
Oxnard, CA 93030
805-487-4961

Western Farm Service
1143 Tervin Avenue
Salinas, CA 93901
408-757-5391

Western Farm Service
801 South Grand
San Jacinto, CA 92383
714-654-9301

Western Farm Service
1015 Linda Vista Drive
San Marcos, CA 92069
800-223-4749

Western Farm Service
3321 West Castor Street
Santa Ana, CA 92704

Western Farm Service
1335 West Main Street
Santa Maria, CA 93454
805-925-8394

Western Farm Service
Highways 33 & 134
Vernalis, CA 95385

Western Farm Service
405 West Beach Street
Watsonville, CA 95076
408-724-2201

Wilbur Ellis Company
696 Naples Street
Chula Vista, CA 92011
619-422-5321

Wilbur Ellis Company
PO Box 1286
Fresno, CA 93715

Wilbur Ellis Company
105 Mercury Circle
Pomona, CA 91768
714-595-4561

Wilbur Ellis Company
6969 Eastside Road
Redding, CA 96001
916-241-9617

Wilbur Ellis Company
20750 Spence Road
Salinas, CA 92401
408-758-1397

Colorado

American Clayworks
857 Bryant Street
Denver, CO 80204
303-534-4044
Toll Free   800-873-2297

Harry Sharp & Son
281 East 55th Avenue
Denver, CO 80216

Western Gard'N-Wise
11600 East 51st Avenue
Denver, CO 80239

Connecticut

Griffen Greenhouse Supplies, Inc.
Wallingford   203-265-0919

W.H. Milikowski
45 Chestnut Hill
Stafford Springs, CT 06076
203-763-3220
Toll Free   800-243-7170

Delaware

Mid Atlantic Plant Co.
Newark   302-366-0349

Florida

Diamond R
PO Box 12489
Ft. Pierce, FL 34981

Diamond R
PO Box 771137
Wintergarden, FL 34777

Florida Growers Supply
Lake Worth   407-968-5039

189

Gonzales Nursery
7460 Pine Forest Road
Pensacola, FL 32526

Howard's Fertilizer
PO Box 593800
Orlando, FL 32859

J.R. Johnson
PO Box 209
Sun City, FL 33586
 813-645-4666

National Polymers, Inc.
Apopka   407-889-4995
Toll Free   800-331-5092

Southern AG.
PO Box 218
Palmetto, FL 34220

Speedling, Incorporated
Sun City   800-881-4769

Terra/Asgrow Company
4144 Highway 39 North
Plant City, FL 33566

United Agri Products
3632 Queen Palm Drive
Tampa, FL 33619

Universal Enterprises
Pompano Beach, FL 33060
Pompano Beach 305-979-0600
Sarasota   813-355-8505

Universal Enterprises
2050 - 51st Street
Sarasota, FL 33508

V.J. Growers Supply
Apopka   407-886-5555
Toll Free   800-327-5422
Toll Free(Fl) 800-432-6925
Lake Worth   407-966-8855
Toll Free   800-432-2483
Homestead   305-378-0497
Toll Free   800-346-8469

Georgia

Atlas Greenhouses
Route 1, Box 339
Alapaha, GA 31622

Florida Seed
2305 Industrial Way
Vidalia, GA 30474

Gavin Horticultural Supply Co.
Albany   912-436-2611
Toll Free   800-741-3349
GROSouth
257 DeKalb Industrial Way
Decatur, GA 30030

GROSouth, Inc.
Tucker, GA   404-938-1881

Graco Fertilizer
PO Box 89
Cairo, GA 31728

Progress Growers Supply
159 Railroad
Canton, GA 30114
 404-479-5528
Toll Free   800-666-4178

Tri-Chek Seed
PO Box 5280
Augusta, GA 30916

Hawaii

A.L.Kilgo, Co., Inc.
Honolulu   808-832-2200

Brewer Environmental
60 Kuhio Road
Hilo, HI 96720
808-961-6061

Brewer Environmental
2910 Beach Road
Maui, HI 96732
808-244-3761

Brewer Environmental
311 Pacific Street
Oahu, HI 96810
808-532-7400

HGP, Inc.
761 Kahoelehau Street
Hawaii, HI 96720
808-935-9304

HGP, Inc.
325 Hukilike Street #6
Kahului, HI 96732
808-877-6636

Idaho

Potlatch Corporation
PO Box 1016
Lewiston, ID 83501
208-799-0123

United Horticultural Supply
PO Box 1196
Caldwell, ID 83606
208-454-0475

Wilbur Ellis Company
Highway 19 & Pinto Road
Caldwell, ID 83605
208-459-1631

Illinois

Ball Seed Co.
West Chicago   708-231-3500

CD Ford
Route 5, PO Box 300
Geneseo, IL 61254

Florist Products
2242 North Palmer Drive
Schaumburg, IL 60173

Florist Products, Inc.
East Dundee, IL   708-428-8828
Toll Free   800-828-2242

J.G. Smith & Co., Inc.
Batavia , IL   708-879-0656

P.A. Bonvallet's Sons
St. Anne , IL   815-427-8222

Siemer Distributers
6300 Collinsville Road
East St. Louis, IL 62201

Siemer Distributors
PO Box 580
Teutopolis, IL 62467

Vaughan's Seed Co.
Downers Grove 708-969-6300
Toll Free   800-323-7253

Yaeger's Distributing Co.
De Kalb   815-756-6005

Indiana

Carl O. Brehob & Sons
3821 Brehob Road
Indianapolis, IN 46217
317-784-1442

Knox County Seed Co.
Vincennes   812-882-0210

Iowa

Consumer Supply
51125 East Richland Street
Storm Lake, IA 50588
712-732-2922
Toll Free   800-274-6810

Kansas

Robert S. Wise
1515 East 29th Street North
Wichita, KS 67219

Swecker Knipp
900 North Jackson
Topeka, KS 66608

Kentucky

Bunton Seed
939 East Jefferson
Louisville, KY 40206
502-584-0136

George W. Hill
8010 Dixie Highway
Florence, KY 41042
606-371-8423

Lose Brothers
4530 Poplar Level Road
Louisville, KY 40213
502-964-6405

Premium Seed Horticultural Supply
915 East Jefferson
Louisville, KY 40206
502-582-3897

Louisiana

Louisiana Nursery Supply (BWI)
11682 Highway 165 South
Forrest Hill, LA 71430
318-748-6361
Toll Free   800-242-7234

V.J. Growers
10462 Highway 165 North
Forest Hill, LA 71430
318-748-6848
Toll Free   800-992-2059

Maine

Griffen Greenhouse Supplies, Inc.
Portland   207-797-0053

Maryland

Maryland Plants & Supplies
Baltimore   410-687-3885

Meyer Seed Co.
Baltimore   410-342-4224

Massachusetts

Griffen Greenhouse Supply
PO Box 36
1619 Main Street
Tewksbury, MA 01876
508-851-4346

Michigan

BFG Supply Co.
Belleville   313-485-7771
Toll Free   800-883-2234
Jenison   616-669-3430

Farmers Co-op Elevator Co.
Hudsonville   616-669-1117

Vriesland Growers Co-op
Hudsonville   616-669-3120

J. Mollema & Son
5400 - 36th Street SE
Grand Rapids, MI 49512
616-940-1441
Toll Free   800-234-4769

Minnesota

J.R. Johnson Supply
2582 Long Lake Road
St. Paul, MN 55113

J.R. Johnson Supply, Inc.
Roseville   612-636-1330

Minnesota Dist. & Mfg., Inc.
1500 Jackson Street NE
Minneapolis, MN 55413
612-781-6068

National Polymers, Inc.
Lakeville   612-469-4977
Toll Free   800-328-4577

Mississippi

BWI - Jackson
PO Box 20407
Jackson, MS 39289
601-922-5214

Terra International
203 Wisteria Drive
Hattiesburg, MS 39401

Terra International
PO Drawer B
Marks, MS 38646

Missouri

BWI of Springfield, Inc.
Springfield   417-881-3003
Toll Free   800-247-4954

Campbell Distributers
1700 West Walnut
Springfield, MO 65806

Ceramo Co. Inc .
Hwy. 72W, PO Box 384
Jackson, MO 63755
314-243-3138

192

Chesmore Seed
5030 Highway 36
St. Joseph, MO 64507
816-279-0865

Hummert International
2746 Chouteau
St. Louis, MO 63103
314-771-0646

Tobin Standard Seed
931 West 8th Street
Kansas City, MO 64101

Montana

Gardner Distributing
6840 Trade Center Avenue
Billings, MT 59104
406-656-5000

McCalif Growers Supplies, Inc.
Billings   406-656-6428

Midland Implement Company
402 Daniels St.
Billings, MT 59102
406-248-7771

Plum Creek Timber Company
PO Box 188
Pablo, MT 59855
406-675-2610

Nebraska

Pioneer Chemical
P.O. Box 921
North Butte,, NE 69101

Nevada

Reno Ranch & Sprinkler
11600 South Virginia Street
Reno, NV 89502
702-852-5022

New Jersey

Growers Supply Co.
Vineland   609-696-2699

Penn State Seed
1508 Route 206
Mount Holly, NJ 08060
609-265-8600

New Mexico

Greenhouse and Garden Supply
3820 Midway Place NE
Albuquerque, NM 87109

New York

Fred C. Gloeckner & Co.
Harrison   914-698-2300

Gardner's Seed Co.
Albany   518-434-6521
Toll Free   800-828-9900

Geiger
Williams & Pearl
Port Chester, NY 10573
914-937-6565

Green Island Distributor
Ridge   516-727-4993

Griffen Greenhouse Supply
4 Cornell Road
Latham, NY 12110
518-786-3500
Toll Free (NY) 800-888-0054

Griffen Greenhouse Supply
Auburn   315-255-1450
Toll Free (NY) 800-500-1450

Penn State Seed Co.
Avon   716-226-6270

Syracuse Farm Supply
Syracuse   315-422-8027

North Carolina

B.J. Williamson, Inc.
Clinton   919-592-6121
Toll Free   800-752-2954

Jeffreys Seed Company
1710 South Highway 117
Goldsboro, NC 27530

Penagro, Inc.
PO Box 608 DTS
Boone, NC 28607

Royster-Clark
495 West St. James Street
Tarboro, NC 27886

Southern Ag
PO Box 85
Boone, NC 28607

Southern Ag.
PO Box 429
Hendersonville, NC 28739

V.J. Growers
4941 Chastain Avenue
Charlotte, NC 28217
704-525-7723
Toll Free   800-222-4504
Toll Free (NC) 800-222-4503

Wyatt Quarles Seed
PO Box 739
Garner, NC 27529

Ohio

BFG Supply
PO Box 479
Burton, OH 44021
216-834-1883
Toll Free   800-883-0234

Cleveland Floral Products
Cleveland   216-676-8521

Garden Aid
PO Box 2006
Dayton, OH 45417

Waldo & Associates, Inc.
Perrysburg   419-666-3662
Toll Free   800-468-4011

Oklahoma

American Plant Products
9200 Northwest 10th
Oklahoma City, OK 73127
405-787-4833
Toll Free   800-522-3376

Oregon

Central Garden & Pet Supply
16179 SE 98th
Clackamas, OR 97015
503-650-4400

McCalif Growers Supplies, Inc.
Hubbard   503-982-1421
Toll Free   800-777-0891

Nurserymen's Supply
4415 North Pacific Highway
Hubbard, OR 97032
503-982-2007

OBC Northwest
Canby   503-266-2021
Portland   503-222-7239
Toll Free   800-477-4744

Teufel Nursery, Inc.
12345 Barnes Road
Portland, OR 97229
503-646-1111

Teufel Products Company
13131 NW Laidlaw
Portland, OR 97299
503-629-2109

United Horticultural Supply
4560 Ridge Drive NE
Salem, OR 97303
503-390-9473

Wilbur Ellis Compnay
3145 Northwest Yeon Street
Portland, OR 97208
503-227-3535

Western Farm Service, Inc.
2883 Industrial Avenue
Hubbard, OR 97032
503-982-3391

Pennsylvania

Brighton By Products
PO Box 23
New Brighton, PA 15066
412-846-1220

D & L Grower Supplies, Inc.
Leola   716-656-0809

E.C. Geiger
Harleysville 800-443-4437

Geiger Corporation
PO Box 285, Route 63
Harleysville, PA 19438
215-256-6511

Henry F. Michell Co.
King of Prussia 215-265-4200
Toll Free   800-422-4678

Penn State Seed Co.
Box 390, Route 309
Dallas, PA 18612
717-675-8585
Toll Free 800-847-7333

Penn State Seed Co.
Bird-in-Hand
717-295-9808

Wetsel Seed Company
PO Box 956
Kittanning, PA 16201
412-545-7181
Toll Free   800-742-2510

South Carolina

Dillon Seed Company
Highway 301 South
Dillon, SC 29536

Park Seed
PO Box 31 Cooksbury
Greenwood, SC 29536

Piedmont Farms
PO Box 4374
Spartanburg, SC 29305
803-576-4524

Tennessee

BWI - Memphis
4403 Delp
Memphis, TN 38180-0390
901-367-2941
Toll Free   800-489-8837

Knoxville Seed
500 Rutledge Pike
Knoxville, TN 37914
615-524-2734
Toll Free   800-264-4968

Mize Farm and Garden
PO Box 3186
Johnson City, TN 37602
615-434-1810
Toll Free   800-321-8161

Sonne-Gro
Knoxville   615-546-9608

Terra International
5018 Highway 41 North
Springfield, TN 31772

Texas

BWI of Dallas, Inc.
Dallas   214-242-4755
Metro   214-988-7548
Toll Free   800-752-6632

BWI - Houston
1229 North Post Oak Road
Houston, TX 77055

BWI - Schulenburg
PO Box 459
Schulenburg, TX 78956
409-743-4581
Toll Free   800-460-9713

BWI - Texarkana
PO Box 990
Nash, TX 75569
903-838-8561
Toll Free   800-527-8612
Toll Free (TX) 800-442-8443

Esco Corporation
2701 East 3rd Street
PO Box 31150
Amarillo, TX 79104

Esco Corporation
12308 Waterton Park Circle
Austin, TX 78726-4000

Esco Corporation
514 West 25th Street
Houston, TX 77008

195

Esco Corporation
103 South Main, PO Box 477
McGregor, TX 76657

Esco Corporation
323 West Expressway
PO Box 838
Pharr, TX 78577

Esco, Ltd.
PO Box 6467
Corpus Christi, TX 78411

Esco, Ltd.
11418 Denton Drive
Dallas, TX 75229

Esco, Ltd.
514 West 25th Street
Houston, TX 77008

Esco, Ltd.
4410 Dividend
San Antonio, TX 78219

Esco, Ltd.
404 North Main
Schulenburg, TX 78956

Gard'N-Wise
Route 1, PO Box 900
1400 East Loop 289
Lubbock, TX 79401

Kinney Bonded Warehouse
102 North 13th Street
Donna, TX 78537

National Polymers, Inc.
San Antonio   210-661-8438
Toll Free   800-221-6365

Sharp & Son
PO Box 10
Schulenburg, TX 78956

Speedling, Incorporated
Alamo   210-787-1911

V.J. Growers
PO Box 1647
Jacksonville, TX 75766
903-586-5858
Toll Free   800-235-0491

Utah

Central Garden & Pet Supply
3756 West 1820 South
Salt Lake City, UT 84104
801-973-7514

United Horticultural Supply
118 East 12675 South
Draper, UT 84020
801-572-6848

Western Gard'n-Wise, Inc.
2790 South 170 West
Salt Lake City, UT 84115
801-487-6200

Wilbur Ellis Company
1345 North 100 East
Spanish Fork, UT 84460
801-798-8643

Virginia

Wetsel Seed Company
PO Box 791
Harrisonburg, VA 22801
703-434-6753

Wetsel Seed Company
PO Box 5189
Virginia Beach, VA 23455
804-460-5634

Washington

Colville Tribal Forestry
PO Box 328
Nespelem, WA 98011
509-634-4661

Environmental Turf Prod.
15720 - 104th Avenue NE
Bothell, WA 98011
206-488-8516

McConkey Company
1615 Puyallup Street
Sumner, WA 98390
206-863-8111

Sharp & Son
900 Lind Avenue SE
Renton, WA 98055
206-235-4510

Steuber Distributing Company
3rd & Pine Street
Snohomish, WA 98290
206-568-2626
Toll Free   800-426-8815
Toll Free (WA) 800-632-8724

United Horticultural Supply
12714-B Valley Avenue East
Sumner, WA 98390
206-863-6327

Wilbur Ellis Company
1521 - 15th Street NW, Suite 5
Auburn, WA 98001
206-441-8927

Wilbur Ellis Company
East 12001 Empire Way
Spokane, WA 99206
509-928-4512

Wisconsin

Carlin Sales
8964 North 51st Street
Milwaukee, WI 53223
 414-355-2300
Toll Free   800-657-0745

Schroth Wholesale Supply Co., Inc.
Menasha   414-722-8101

Remember, companies can change telephone numbers and addresses, and the telephone companies are changing area codes throughout the country.

GLOSSARY

air pruning: roots of plants in open end sleeves cease to grow downward upon reaching the bottom of the container when they come into contact with air and spread laterally instead, thus developing a more fibrous root system.

annual: a plant whose entire life cycle is completed in one year or less.

asexual reproduction: propagation by plant tissue, not by seed or spore.

B & B: Balled and Burlapped, field grown plants which are dug from the ground; the soil of the rootball is wrapped in burlap to keep it intact.

bar code: the universal product binary code symbol for computer scanning.

bareroot: a condition in which a plant is shipped or sold with no soil around the root system.

bedding plant: usually a small annual flowering plant sold in packs or flats, such as marigolds and petunias.

biennial: a plant which only lives two years.

blighted: a plant affected by a fungus or viral disease which produces withering of leaves especially on the growing tips of the plant.

broker: a middleman who represents a number of different nursery clients.

budding: the formation of flower or leaf buds; also a grafting term for inserting budwood into a rootstock.

caliper: the diameter of a plant's trunk usually measured at or near the ground line.

certified farmers market: a farmers market where the produce has been grown by the people who are selling it.

certified viral free: usually refers to fruiting trees and vines which are certified to have been produced from virus free budwood.

climate zone: an area where the same general climate conditions apply. The USDA has divided the country into different zones indicating average minimum temperatures. A plant's cold hardiness is referenced by the zone number. Other publications such as the *Sunset Western Garden Book* break the areas into even more specific localized zones.

color / color spot: blooming bedding plants.

common name: the name the plant is most commonly known by, usually not the Latin name.

compost: a broad term for any wide ranging combination of organic materials which has been allowed to decompose over a period of time.

conifer: any variety of plant which produces its seed in a cone.

consignment: placing a product with vendors with the agreement that they pay you only for what sells with return privileges for the rest.

crooked: describes a tree which has a bend in the trunk.

cross pollination: the pollen from one plant fertilizes the seeds of another plant of the same family.

cultivars: a contraction of "cultivated variety"; a group of plants distinguished by certain characteristics which they maintain when reproduced.

cuttings: plant tissue cut into pieces for placement into rooting media in order to propagate new plants.

damping off: a fungus disease which kills newly germinated seedlings.

deciduous: describes a plant which loses its leaves in the winter season.

deferred billing: a selling inducement giving the retailer extra time to sell material before having to pay for it.

defoliate: to lose leaves.

die-back: a portion of a plant dies from disease or frost damage without killing the whole plant.

die down: refers to an herbaceous perennial whose top growth dies to the ground going into winter and regenerates from the roots in the spring.

division: a propagation method whereby a large plant is separated into smaller plants.

dormant: used of deciduous plants when they have lost their leaves, literally means "sleeping."

drip system: an automatic irrigation system with water emitters placed directly at the base of the plant delivering usually one to two gallons per hour.

dumping: as a selling term it means to sell material at very low prices.

dwarf: a plant which is the smallest in any given species either by nature or by hybridizing or by grafting onto less aggressive rootstocks.

evergreen: any plant which does not shed all its foliage in a season.

flat: a shallow plastic tray used to hold bedding or ground cover plants.

FOB: "free on board," a shipping term meaning that the material is loaded onto the truck for free, "FOB point of origin" means that the transportation charges to destination are extra, "FOB destination" means that the shipping charges are included.

forest seedlings: conifer tree seedlings, such as fir, spruce, pine, redwood and cedar.

frost tender: sensitive to temperatures below freezing with potential for damage or death.

fungicide: a chemical used to kill fungus diseases.

future order: an advance order, usually for spring inventory, reserved for a customer and shipped later with deferred billing.

germinate: to sprout seeds.

graft union: the place where the root stock and the scion meet.

green goods: plant material sold in retail nurseries.

ground cover: a type of low, usually fast spreading perennial plant used to cover large areas of ground.

hard goods: all material other than plants sold in retail nurseries.

harden off: to transfer plants from a warm greenhouse environment to an intermediate cooler yet protected location in order to make the tender growth more tolerant of the true outside conditions.

hose-end sprayer: a sprayer which attaches to the end of a hose and works with water pressure rather than air pressure as in tank sprayers.

hybrid: a plant distinctly different from its parents produced by cross pollination of different species or varieties.

injection fertilization: a method to feed plants as you water with fertilizer already injected into the nursery's water system.

invoice: a billing statement requesting payment for the products listed.

lath house: a protective structure whose frame is covered with thin slats of wood with spacing between, offering shade and some frost protection.

liner: refers either to the small 2" pots or the plants grown in the 2" pots for the purpose of replanting into larger containers.

N-P-K: the three major active ingredients in fertilizer, nitrogen, phosphorus and potassium written in a series of three numbers in that order indicating the percentage of each in the fertilizer.

native: a plant which is found growing naturally in the local area.

net 30 days: an invoice term meaning that the bill is due in full in 30 days with no discount. When a discount is offered for fast payment it is written 2% discount 10 days, net 30, meaning that if the bill is paid in 10 days the customers can take a 2% discount, but if he waits the 30 days, the amount is due in full.

node: the joint in a stem from which a leaf bud grows.

non-selective: used of chemicals which indiscriminately kill whatever weed or insect with which they come in contact.

organic: used to describe the production of plants, fruits and vegetables without the use of industrial chemicals, also used to describe non-synthetic fertilizers or insect controls.

overgrown one: a one gallon plant which is much larger than the normally marketed size making it more desirable for transplanting into a five gallon can.

packaged bareroot: bareroot plants placed in plastic bags with a medium to keep the roots moist, thus giving them a longer shelf life in the stores.

patent tag: a label accompanying any plant which has been patented by its creator containing a warning against asexual reproduction and thus protecting the rights to royalties from its sale.

perennial: any plant whose life cycle extends beyond two years, but it is also used generically to describe herbaceous flowering plants.

pesticide: any chemical used to kill insects, fungus or weeds.

picture tag: a label which contains the plant's picture as well as its name and perhaps a description.

pinch back: to prune a plant by pinching off the tips.

plug: an annual or perennial seedling with a very small rootball designed to be transplanted or "plugged" into a larger pot.

pre-emergent: a chemical control used to kill weed seeds as they germinate.

propagation: the reproduction of plants by any method, including seed, cuttings or grafting.

prune: to trim a plant, usually for shaping.

purchase order: the buyer's paperwork authorizing the purchase and shipping of your order.

quarantine: a restriction on the movement and sale of plants within a given area.

resale: to resell to the public the products purchased from the wholesaler.

rootball: the soil area in which the roots of the plant are contained.

root bound: when the roots have become so tight or circling in the container that little or no soil is visible.

root crown: the highest point on the trunk where there are roots, for planting bareroot this represents the ground line.

root stock: in grafted material the plant which is used for the root system.

rose pot: a small liner pot 2 1/4" wide and 3 1/4" deep.

Round-up™: a trademarked non-selective weed killer.

runner: a stem coming from the base of a perennial from which new plants root naturally.

scion: the tissue which is grafted onto the rootstock.

seasonal: suited to the season, in plant sales it refers to the peak time of the year when the majority of the sales are made for any given type of plants, e.g.. bedding plants in spring, shade trees in fall.

seedling: any young plant which was started from seed.

sexual reproduction: plants produced from pollinized seeds or spores.

shade cloth: a woven fabric which blocks out a high percentage of the sun's rays, used to provide shade for sun sensitive plants.

shifting: to transplant from a smaller container into a larger.

sleeve: a type of pot which is narrow across the top and deep with a taper to the bottom.

slip: a cutting.

specialty plants: plants which have been trained into special forms or trellised.

specimen: usually refers to a tree or shrub in a fifteen gallon container or larger.

spiked: on plants which produce flowers on long stems, such as agapanthus and daylilies, it means having a flower ready to bloom.

standard: the largest size of any tree; also any shrub trained into a tree form.

sterilization: the chemical process of making field soil free from disease and weeds; in potting soils this process is usually achieved by heating the soil.

stone fruit: any type of fruit which has a pit, such as peaches or nectarines.

stratify: a preparatory process for germinating hard coated seeds by placing in different levels of soil and holding at cold temperatures until planting.

systemic: a type of chemical which is absorbed into a plant's system and remains there as a poison for insects and disease control; never to be used on food crops.

tie-off: to reserve a block of plants for a particular customer.

time release fertilizer: a resin coated fertilizer which releases its nutrients slowly over a period of time.

tip prune: to cut off the ends of branches.

top dressing: to add fertilizer on the top of the soil in a container.

topiary: plants trained into particular shapes or forms, especially animals or geometric shapes.

topped: refers to a tree which has had its central leader cut back.

untopped: refers to a tree which has not had its leader cut back.

USDA: United States Department of Agriculture.

water wand: a long tube attached to a hose with a sieve at the end to diffuse the force of the water.

weed cloth: a porous woven fabric which is laid on the ground to prevent weeds from sprouting.

wet feet: a condition caused by water standing on the roots of a plant, cutting off oxygen and thereby killing the roots.

whip: a young tree which has not yet developed any lateral branches at the top.

INDEX